Mozambique's Samora Machel

OHIO SHORT HISTORIES OF AFRICA

This series of Ohio Short Histories of Africa is meant for those who are looking for a brief but lively introduction to a wide range of topics in African history, politics, and biography, written by some of the leading experts in their fields.

Mozambique's Samora Machel

A Life Cut Short

Allen F. Isaacman

Barbara S. Isaacman

Foreword by Albie Sachs

OHIO UNIVERSITY PRESS

ATHENS

Ohio University Press, Athens, Ohio 45701
ohioswallow.com
© 2020 by Ohio University Press
All rights reserved

Printed in the United States of America
Ohio University Press books are printed on acid-free paper ⊚ ™

30 29 28 27 26 25 24 23 22 21 20   5 4 3 2 1

Library of Congress Cataloging-in-Publication Data
Names: Isaacman, Allen F., author. | Isaacman, Barbara, author. | Sachs,
  Albie, 1935- writer of foreword.
Title: Mozambique's Samora Machel : a life cut short / Allen F. Isaacman,
  Barbara S. Isaacman ; foreword by Albie Sachs.
Other titles: Ohio short histories of Africa.
Description: Athens : Ohio University Press, [2020] | Series: Ohio short
  histories of Africa | Includes bibliographical references and index.
Identifiers: LCCN 2020016049 | ISBN 9780821424230 (paperback) | ISBN
  9780821446942 (pdf)
Subjects: LCSH: Machel, Samora, 1933-1986. | Presidents--Mozambique--20th
  century--Biography. | Nationalists--Mozambique--Biography. |
  Mozambique--Politics and government--To 1975. | Mozambique--Politics and
  government--1975-1994.
Classification: LCC DT3393.M33 I73 2020 | DDC 967.9051092--dc23
LC record available at https://lccn.loc.gov/2020016049

To the Mozambican people

Contents

Illustrations

Foreword

The words "*A luta continua*" appear in an artwork next to the doors of South Africa's Constitutional Court, which stands in the heart of the Old Fort Prison. They remind us of leaders like M. K. Gandhi, Albert Luthuli, Nelson and Winnie Mandela, Helen Joseph, Fatima Meer, Oliver Tambo, and Robert Sobukwe who were locked up there for their pursuit of justice and freedom. To this day, when people in South Africa challenge corruption and abuse of office in high places, they say, "*A luta continua!*" The struggle continues! The phrase reminds us of our connection with Mozambique and with Samora Machel. It brings back to me the inspiration I received from Samora during the eleven years I lived and worked in that country and nearly died there.

How we loved to hear Samora speak to vast crowds in Independence Square. He was funny, melodious, entrancing, conveying big political ideas with clarity and simplicity. You always learned something. You felt connected with him and with tens of thousands of others listening avidly to every word.

And how he delighted us with his invocations of internationalism. He constantly reminded the thousands filling the square that Mozambique had gained its independence with enormous international support and that people from all over the world were welcome to cooperate in building a new society. In the crowd I would see scores of people from a multitude of countries. Among them would be Cubans sent by Fidel, Chileans who had escaped from Pinochet, and Brazilians and Argentinians who had evaded the military dictatorships in their countries. There were South Africans—Ruth First, before she was assassinated, Alpheus Manghezi and Rob Davies from the Centre for African Studies, me from the newly created law school at Eduardo Mondlane University, and students like Ben Mokoena and Tom Moyane. And there would be Allen Isaacman, preeminent historian of contemporary Mozambique, and his wife Barbara Isaacman, my colleague at the law school (the "Isaacpeople," as we jokingly called them), the authors of this magnificently researched and most compelling book.

We all felt proud to be there. Samora would lead us in singing freedom songs, and then in the "vivas": "Long live the just struggle of the oppressed people of South Africa!"—"Viva!" "Long live the emancipation of women!"—"Viva!" "Down with racism, tribalism, and regionalism!"—"*Abaixo!*" "*A luta. . .,*" Samora would declaim and pause, and we would respond, "*continua!*"

We especially loved Samora's humor and sense of humanity. Referring to Africa's homegrown exploiters, he would tell us there were people who would fiercely resist being eaten by a foreign tiger but not mind at all being devoured by a local lion. Discussing relations with countries like Zambia and Tanzania, he would observe that there were people in neighboring countries who thought they were superior because they had been colonized by the British and not the Portuguese. Or he might ask, Why was it that in colonial times our waiters would serve the Portuguese soldiers with courtesy and respect, but now would be rude to their own people? The answer was that the enemy was camping in our heads—we still had the mentality of underdevelopment.

Stories about Samora became legend. I remember how inspired I was by the tale of an exchange between Samora and his father. In the colonial period, Samora's father was expelled from a fertile piece of land along the Limpopo River to make way for Portuguese peasants to grow rice there. When independence came and the colonists returned to Portugal, Papa Machel asked his son when he could go back and start planting there again. To his dismay and to our delight, Samora replied that Frelimo had not fought for the president's father to get land, but for the nation to get food. Our joy was unmitigated.

We believed that the beneficiaries of the revolution should be those in greatest need, rather than those close to the president, and that private ownership of land should give way to more collectivized, socialist forms of land use. With Bulgarian help, the Frelimo government created a huge state farm on the banks of the Limpopo. Tractors came to till the soil, which was good, but they put in too much fertilizer, which was bad. The rice grew too quickly and volunteers from the towns were needed to harvest the premature crop. Now, if anybody asks me to come and cut rice, even when it was before the bomb and I still had two arms, I know they are in desperate straits. Even if for me it was fantastic to be out in the fields with the workers cutting rice with a sickle, for the country it was a disaster. Our delight turned to dismay. The objective was noble and, given the absence of an indigenous managerial class, the temptation to place everything in state hands was understandable. But the result was calamitous. Today, not even the most radical thinkers would deny that Samora's father should have gotten back his land, not because he was the president's father, but because he had been forced off it in the first place.

This happy story turned sad reminds me of one of Samora's favorite sayings: to know the taste of an avocado pear, you must cut it in half. By this he meant that instead of attempting to suppress political contradictions, you should bring them out into the open, deal with them decisively, and emerge stronger as a result. This book is packed with carefully sourced and compactly presented information dealing with many of the contradictions with which Frelimo had to grapple.

I had long known about the struggle between two lines inside Frelimo in its early days, how Samora had ardently supported nonracialism in the ranks, refused to kill captured Portuguese soldiers, assisted Josina Machel in her determination to bear arms, and insisted that the enemy was not a race but a system of exploitation. I was also familiar with the way Frelimo artfully navigated the difficult waters of the Cold War. But in page after page of this book, I discovered new information. I learned about the fragmented state of Frelimo at the time its founder Eduardo Mondlane was assassinated, of intense later debates in the Frelimo leadership, about details of the Matola Raid by Pretoria's commandos, of how the Nkomati Accord with Botha came to be signed, about the killing of Simango and others who had been expelled from Frelimo, and, finally, fascinating details about Samora as a caring, loving, but stern father of five children.

I was, of course, familiar with the fierce contradiction between newly independent Mozambique, constructed on notions of people's power, and its neighbor, racist South Africa, built on the premise of white supremacy. I knew much about South Africa's determination to destabilize all the Frontline States, Mozambique and Angola in particular. But I was surprised to discover the immensity of the price that Mozambique paid for supporting our liberation struggle.

When Pretoria mouthed military threats, claiming Mozambique had secret weapons from the Soviet Union, Samora responded that his country's secret weapons were people like Ruth First, who, for her belief in human dignity and justice for all, had been killed by a letter bomb from South Africa sent to her at the Centre for African Studies. Yet Pretoria's aggression against Mozambique went well beyond Ruth First's assassination and the killing of other ANC members in the country.

It involved provoking and fanning the flames of civil war. South African commandos regularly sabotaged electricity lines. When South African musician Abdullah Ibrahim gave a memorial piano recital for Ruth on the night of her death, all the lights in the city went out, and Abdullah's musical homage continued memorably with a single candle burning. A bridge over the Zambezi River was blown up. Ships from abroad and trains from the interior of Africa would be rerouted away from Maputo Harbor. There were millions of refugees. The economy was never able to achieve liftoff. Scores of children were recruited by Renamo as soldiers in the fight against Frelimo. Hundreds of thousands of people died. Thousands more lost limbs to land mines. Though I survived the bomb placed in my car by agents of South African security, losing my right arm and the sight of one eye, two Mozambicans died from shrapnel injuries.

Some of the most powerful passages in this book deal with the way the plane carrying Samora, his assistant Fernando Honwana, director of the Centre for African Studies Aquino de Braganca, and more than twenty others was lured to destruction on South African soil. It was bringing them back from a meeting of some of the Frontline States in Zambia, undertaken to reinforce the opposition to Pretoria. We were stunned in Mozambique. We wept openly. A week before the crash, Rob Davies, who listened to the SABC *Current Affairs* propaganda broadcast every morning, had prepared a report to be sent to Oliver Tambo in Lusaka indicating that he had noted a profound shift in Pretoria's stance with regard to Samora Machel. Until that week, he pointed out, the line from Pretoria had been that Samora must be rescued from the claws of his communist controllers. Now the broadcaster said that Samora had shown himself to be the enemy of good neighborliness in the region and the back of his power had to be broken. Days later, Samora died.

Samora often spoke about the People—*o Povo*. "The People never die," he would tell us. "Leaders come and leaders go, but the People never die." And now

Samora was dead. The people were to endure several more years of bitter civil war, thousands more were to die, and hundreds more would lose their legs to land mines. The energy and optimism that marked the revolution and the nation's founding had been destroyed. New problems of corruption and authoritarianism were to emerge.

And then, in the strange way in which history works, as beautifully captured here, the indomitable spirit of Samora began to emerge once more. This time it was not through his songs and speeches as head of state in Independence Square, but through cassettes and rap music listened to by people on the ground. And so it came to pass that it was the memory of Samora in the minds of the people that never died.

Our thanks must go to Allen and Barbara for capturing so much of this remarkable story. Allen the idealist and Barbara the sceptic joined forces to provide us with a portrait of a great African leader that is rich, loving, and incisive. The book reminds us how interdependent the peoples of Africa have been and must continue to be. It reveals the terrible price in blood and treasure that Mozambique was forced to pay before we in South Africa were able to bring apartheid down. It shows how Mozambique became a crucible for political development in our part of the world, teaching us the importance of having good leadership and leaders rather than a single great leader. Above all, it calls upon us to continue Samora's quest to transform our society and economy in favor of the poor and the marginalized, but to do so through the complex and constitutionally defined mechanisms of an open and democratic society.

This was a lesson those of us living and working in Mozambique learned not from books or ideology, but from experience.

Samora was a proud African, a proud liberator, a proud internationalist, and a proud and humane human being with great cultural sensibility. He had his faults, and the system in which he grew and that he helped to grow had its deficiencies. But flaws and all, *o Povo*, the People, are right to revere his memory. My generation honors and loves him for the way he transformed the nature of what an African revolutionary leader could be. He indigenized revolutionary theory, fought against racism and tribalism, and spoke passionately about the emancipation of women. He is loved by ordinary people in Mozambique today for epitomizing qualities they fail to see in most current leaders: his integrity, his warm, engaging, and culturally rich humanity, his independence of mind and spirit, and, above all, his profound and resolute determination to enable the poor to transform their lives.

Viva Samora Machel, viva! May the struggle for which he gave his life continue! *A luta continua!*

Albie Sachs
Cape Town

Acknowledgments

We owe a special debt of gratitude to numerous Mo-
zambican friends and colleagues who, over the years,
have taught us so much about their country's history.
Special thanks to Yusuf Adam Azagáia, Isabel María Casimiro, Arlindo Chilundo, João Paulo Borges Coelho,
Frances Christie, Flávia Gemio, Eulésio Viegas Felipe,
Carlos Fernandes, Raul Honwana, Suzette Honwana,
Benedito Machava, Denise Malauene, Ricardo Rangel,
Daniel Ribeiro, Alda Saute, Teresa Cruz e Silva, António
Sopa, Amélia Neves de Souto, Joel Tembe, Carmen Zucula, and Paulo Zucula. Luís Bernardo Honwana, our
close friend, over the years shared with us much of his
family's past, but, as head of the Office of the President
during much of Samora's presidency, he chose not to di-
vulge information about either its inner workings or his
relationship with Samora and the Frelimo leadership.

Without the first-hand knowledge of Aquino de
Bragança, José Luís Cabaço, Iain Christie, Teodato Hunguana, António Alves Gomes, Oscar Monteiro, João
Velemo Nunguanbe, Jacob Jeremias Nyambir, Prakash
Ratilal, Honorata Simão Tschussa, and António Hama,
we would not have been able to write this book. Their
recollections provided invaluable insights on Samora

the man and political leader, and they filled in gaps in our knowledge about the significant forces shaping the trajectory of Mozambican history.

We were fortunate to have the opportunity to speak with members of Samora's immediate family on several occasions. Our conversations were frank and far-reaching, sometimes lasting several hours. Through their story-telling, dating back to Samora's youth, we were able to piece together a better understanding of this complex leader. We especially thank Graça, Olívia, Ornila, Jucelina, and Samito, as well as Samora's nieces and nephews, who made these encounters so informative and enjoyable.

Several prominent scholars of Mozambique read this manuscript carefully and critically. We are particularly indebted to Edward Alpers, Heidi Gengenbach, Paolo Israel, William Minter, David Morton, and Jeanne Penvenne. Their comments made this a far better book, as did the valuable suggestions offered by Paul Fauvet and Elizabeth Schmidt.

We have benefited from the smart and sensitive suggestions from close friends who have accompanied us over the years on our Mozambican journey. To Jim Johnson, Roberta Washington, Sara Evans, Ray Arsenault, and Gillian Berchowitz we owe profound thanks.

We are especially grateful to Daniel Douek, who shared his personal copies of Truth and Reconciliation Commission testimony, to Paolo Israel, who provided songs about Samora he had collected in Cabo Delgado, to the archivists at the Centro de Documentação Samora Machel for the time and energy they devoted to assisting us and the photographs of Samora they shared. The book is also graced with photographs from the Centro de Documentação e Formação Fotográfica.

The University of Minnesota Foundation provided research funds through Allen's Regents Professorship, and the Graduate School helped to fund our overseas research.

We dedicate this book to the people of Mozambique, who, for fifty years, have welcomed us, opened their homes to us, and shared with us recollections of their history.

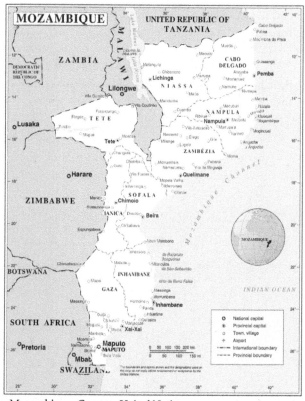

Mozambique. *Courtesy United Nations.*

Prologue

The Challenge of Representation

Samora Machel is remembered as Mozambique's first president and one of a number of assassinated prominent African leaders, such as Patrice Lumumba (Congo), Amílcar Cabral (Guinea-Bissau), and Thomas Sankara (Burkina Faso). For Mozambicans, he was the head of FRELIMO (Frente de Libertação de Moçambique), the guerrilla army that, against great odds, brought freedom to their homeland, but on the international scene he was much more.

Throughout southern Africa, Samora was a hero to the oppressed. His military successes against a colonial regime buttressed by South Africa, Rhodesia, the United States, and its NATO allies enhanced his revolutionary reputation. His support for Zimbabwean liberation forces and the African National Congress, which came at great cost to his nation, further elevated his stature. To the settler government ruling Rhodesia and South Africa's apartheid regime, he was the embodiment of evil—a powerful black man committed to building a nonracialist socialist society on their borders.

Samora also enjoyed international prominence far beyond Mozambique's significance. In 1975, when Mozambique became independent, the world looked appreciably different than it does today. Revolutionary movements with radical socialist agendas were on the rise. Cuba had withstood American efforts to destroy its revolution, the United States had been defeated in Vietnam, the Sandinistas had come to power in Nicaragua, and the winds of change were threatening to sweep away settler governments in southern Africa. Samora was part of a new generation of revolutionary leaders—Fidel Castro, Daniel Ortega, Michael Manley, and Yasser Arafat—with whom he shared a common vision and warm friendships.

For China and Russia, which supported FRELIMO during the armed struggle, Samora was an important ally helping to counter the West's influence in Africa. After independence, however, the Soviets never completely trusted him—he was too independent, refusing to follow the dogmatic Marxist-Leninist line or support Moscow in its battles with Beijing. By contrast, the NATO countries tracked Samora's rise to power with concern. The United States viewed Mozambique through the same Cold War prism as the Soviets, but for Washington he posed a threat to America's growing interest in Africa. Samora also played an important role in the Non-Aligned Movement, where he took a militantly anti-imperialist stance and fervently opposed both Eastern and Western attempts at global hegemony.

By the 1980s, however, Samora's standing, both domestically and internationally, had suffered. Nevertheless, he still posed such a significant threat to the apartheid regime and its allies that South African officials plotted to eliminate him. On October 19, 1986, he died in a mysterious plane crash.

His passing was a terrible loss to the country and the region, as well as for those throughout the world who shared his ideals. We were among them.

We learned of Samora's death the following night, well after midnight in Minneapolis, by a telephone call from Roberta Washington, a dear friend and fellow *cooperante* with whom we had worked closely in Mozambique. In a subdued voice, she told us that Samora Moises Machel and many of his closest advisers had died when the plane carrying them back from Zambia smashed into a mountainside in Mbuzini, South Africa.

During the two years (1978–79) that we lived in Mozambique with our two young sons, we had gotten to know Samora, whom we admired greatly, both from afar and through various personal interactions. Among those who lost their lives that night were many close Mozambican friends who were like family to us, including Aquino de Bragança and Fernando Honwana. We mourn their loss to this day.

Our relationship with Mozambique and its people had begun decades earlier. In 1968, we traveled to the then-Portuguese colony so Allen could conduct research for his doctoral dissertation. He had selected Mozambique partly because of his desire to help liberate its past from the cultural arrogance and racist assumptions that framed the colonial representation of the Mozambican people. For too long, their experiences had resided in the shadow of historical scholarship that focused almost exclusively on the Portuguese.

As activists at the University of Wisconsin in the early 1960s committed to social justice, the civil rights movement, the antiwar campaign, and the efforts to dismantle the apartheid regime, the armed struggle being waged by FRELIMO to end centuries of Portuguese oppression intensified our interest in the colony. (In this study, "FRELIMO" refers to the liberation movement and "Frelimo" to the postindependence political party.) Happily, Portuguese authorities were unaware of our politics. We only received clearance because a high-ranking Portuguese official believed we would discover there that Lisbon was pursuing a benign multiracial social experiment known as "luso-tropicalism." Since colonial authorities were convinced that illiterate Africans had no real history and we would only be studying "myths and legends," Allen's research appeared to pose no threat to the status quo.

Once in the interior, however, a sympathetic colonial administrator alerted us that the notorious secret police known as PIDE (Polícia Internacional e de Defesa do Estado) were following us. His warning came after we created a ruckus in the small interior town of Sena, where we were renting a room in the rear of the local bar. In violation of social conventions, we had encouraged our translator to use our bathroom, which we shared with the owner's family, rather than relieving himself outdoors. The owner's wife was furious, publicly berating us about the dangers of allowing uncivilized *pretos* (blacks) to use European bathrooms. The next day, PIDE agents questioned those who had witnessed this exchange. After independence, we discovered that this interrogation was not an isolated incident. In the archives was a lengthy PIDE report describing how PIDE agents had shown up to question the Africans with whom we spoke in every village we visited.

Such an incident, although largely insignificant, revealed the inherently exploitative and degrading nature of Portuguese colonialism. When colonial officials, loyalist chiefs, and known informers were not present, elders across the Zambezi Valley described in detail the abuses experienced on a regular basis.[1] We learned how, under Portugal's forced labor regime (*chibalo*), which the elders characterized as a modern-day form of slavery, colonial administrators compelled Africans to work for six-month periods for little or no pay on public works projects and European plantations, farms, and mines. Those trying to run away were beaten and jailed. Even compliance, however, did not protect them from the overseers' physical abuses. The tattered rags many villagers wore and the malnourished and uneducated children we encountered daily stood in sharp contrast to the luxuries enjoyed by the settler community.

For most Africans living in Lourenço Marques, the colonial capital, or Beira, the colony's second-largest city, life was only marginally better. We regularly witnessed Africans being slapped, humiliated, even arrested for behavior considered inappropriate. We walked through teeming *subúrbios* (shantytowns) crowded with reed huts (*caniços*) that lacked running water, a sewage system, proper drainage, and other basic infrastructure. The cities where Europeans lived were off-limits to almost all Africans except during working hours.[2] The informal but vigorously enforced color bar limited educational and job opportunities for the majority of the African population. Racial intermarriage was frowned upon, although many Europeans frequented the red-light district. All these indignities revealed the true nature of "lusotropicalism."

Of course, a small number of Africans escaped the most dehumanizing colonial practices. We encountered *assimilados* and African bureaucrats with European *padrinhos* (patrons) who had acquired cement houses on the edges of the European cities and were able to provide their children with more than a rudimentary education.[3] Samora's family members were assimilados, as was his widow, Graça Machel, who had been the only African student in her high school class.[4]

The modest economic and social reforms promulgated in the 1960s did not protect Africans from the whims of settlers, although not all Portuguese were abusive. In the privacy of their homes or in quiet cafes, a handful of Portuguese felt comfortable enough to openly criticize the fascist dictatorship of the late António Salazar. Some even acknowledged a certain sympathy for FRELIMO.

We could not remain silent, given the exploitative nature of what we observed during our year in Mozambique. Upon our return to the United States in 1970, Allen met with Sharfudin Khan, FRELIMO representative to the United Nations, to offer support and joined the fledgling Committee for a Free Mozambique. When the book based on his dissertation won the 1974 African Studies Association's Herskovits Prize, he donated a portion of the prize money to FRELIMO and, more importantly, pushed the ASA to condemn Portuguese colonial rule in Mozambique, Angola, Guinea-Bissau, Cabo Verde, and São Tomé. In June 1975, Allen appeared before the US Congress to condemn American support for the Lisbon government, and he subsequently testified at congressional subcommittee hearings on the situation in postindependence Mozambique.

On June 25, 1975, Mozambique, under Frelimo's leadership, gained independence and Samora Machel became its first president. Two years later, we were invited to teach at Eduardo Mondlane University (UEM), named for FRELIMO's first president, who had been assassinated by the Portuguese. The seventeen months we lived there were heady times, despite food shortages and long lines for bread and meat. The children on our block quickly befriended our two sons—partly because they had the only soccer ball in the neighborhood—and we, as well as other cooperantes, were treated as comrades and *progressistas*. Barbara worked for the Mozambican Women's Organization (OMM), wrote a book about the legal position of women in Mozambique as part of the United Nations Decade for Women, and taught labor law at the UEM's law faculty. Allen helped train the first generation of postindependence Mozambican historians. We were energized and committed to participating in the revolution. We believed anything was possible, even if it required us at times to suspend our critical faculties.

Under the auspices of the Office of the President we undertook several projects, including surveying the living and working conditions of Western cooperantes and serving as liaisons with Business International, a Western-based organization promoting investments across the world. Allen and his colleague Iain Christie conducted a five-hour interview with Samora that appeared in several Western newspapers and journals. We also met periodically with President Machel and came away impressed with his energy, intellect, and deep commitment to ending social injustice.

Samora had a wry sense of humor, a big ego, and loved to hold court. On one occasion, the American cooperantes living in Maputo made a donation to help rebuild a village attacked by US mercenaries working for the white settler regime in neighboring Rhodesia. We stood in a receiving line and, as Samora walked by with his entourage, he introduced Barbara as "Allen Isaacman's wife," to which Barbara replied, "No, he is my husband." Samora laughed and nodded approvingly to the entourage accompanying him.

Upon our return home in 1979, we continued to support Mozambique and its socialist project. We organized the Mozambican Education Fund—which to our surprise was granted tax-exempt status by the Internal Revenue Service—through which we sent several thousand badly need books to rural schools established after independence. We also worked closely with Valeriano Ferrão, Mozambique's ambassador to the United States, to mobilize opposition to the increasing aggression of South Africa and its surrogates inside Mozambique.[5]

Barbara returned to Mozambique periodically and was a guest at the 1982 OMM conference. At the Frelimo-organized reception, President Machel greeted her and asked where Allen was. When she told him that her husband was, of course, at home caring for their children, he laughed and responded, "You see, we have something to learn from you Americans." Around the same time, Barbara's book *Women, the Law and Agrarian Change*, co-written with June Stephens, was translated into Portuguese and read widely throughout the country.

For the next several years Allen spent most summers in Mozambique collecting oral histories. At the end of every visit he met with President Machel and other government officials to discuss conditions in the countryside and politics in the United States. While his critique of Frelimo's disregard for rural culture and history sometimes fell on deaf ears—on one occasion a party ideologue dismissed his criticisms as the idealistic views of an "*Africanista*"—Samora always gave his full attention to Allen's accounts of the abuses of power, incompetence, and corruption he had witnessed. Samora made many errors and was quick to anger, but he also demonstrated the capacity to listen, challenge inherited orthodoxies, and engage in self-criticism.

We have sketched our connection with Mozambique and FRELIMO to underscore that we were both students of and witnesses to an important period in Mozambican history. We also hope to show how our interpretation of this history is informed by our personal experiences, politics, and somewhat different temperaments (Barbara was always somewhat more skeptical about FRELIMO's policies than Allen). In some ways, we are telling a life story where the relationship between authors and subjects is inseparable from the story told.[6]

Although we were partisans, we are also scholars who prize intellectual rigor and careful analysis. As engaged scholars, we are committed to challenging social hierarchies and oppressive institutions and the racist assumptions supporting them. Not content to critique the status quo, in our own small way we have sought to change it. We are driven by a mutually reinforcing intellectual and political commitment, and we reject the notion that there is a singular authentic history. Our allegiance to scholarship and activism, however, poses a serious challenge. We recognize the problematic relationships between biographer and subject. Passionate commitments to worldly causes must not undermine the capacity to question or the willingness to criticize the causes and movements we support and the men and women we admire. Edward Said put it bluntly when he cautioned, "never solidarity before criticism."[7]

In this social biography of Samora Machel we have tried to maintain that critical stance and avoid the tendency to romanticize a man we held in high regard. It has not been easy; some may conclude that we have not been successful. While we do not apologize for our stance, readers must recognize that our interpretations of this critical period in Mozambique's history necessarily differ from those of people who criticized FRELIMO's revolutionary agenda or actively opposed it.

In writing this biography, we have consulted both academic publications and a substantial body of unpublished primary material. The Centro de Documentação Samora Machel in Maputo houses a rich collection of Samora's papers and other documents related to his family. The secret police (PIDE) files in the Arquivo Nacional de Torre de Tombo, while generally depicting Samora as a Marxist pawn of China or the Soviet Union, contain voluminous material on the FRELIMO leadership and its strategy. We were not able to review thousands of FRELIMO wartime documents that fell overboard into the Indian Ocean when FRELIMO transferred its office from Dar es Salaam to Maputo, nor the very substantial collection of documents from the armed struggle housed in the FRELIMO archives, which are still not open to the public and would have supported a more comprehensive analysis of Samora's role.[8]

This study also relies on over twenty interviews with figures who had close relationships with Samora, collected by FRELIMO-sanctioned researchers in the wake of Samora's death and now deposited in the archives of the Centro de Documentação. We have also drawn on our interviews of members of his immediate family and several close advisers. To try to avoid the "bias of proximity," we spoke to former guerrilla fighters, peasants, Portuguese settlers, a rap singer, and a Portuguese priest; referenced material we collected in Mozambique over the past half-century; and consulted John Marcum's recently published *Conceiving Mozambique*, which contains detailed oral accounts from disenchanted former members of FRELIMO who studied in the United States. We intended to supplement this information with interviews of prominent Beira residents who were outspoken opponents of Samora, but two days before our scheduled flight to Beira in March 2019, Typhoon Ida devastated the city and surrounding areas, making that impossible.

The oral and written documents we consulted are all social texts that often contain multiple or contradictory meanings. Nostalgia, limits of memory, and the politics of forgetting complicate their construction. We are reminded of the often-cited admonition of the French anthropologist Marc Augé: "tell me what you forget and I will tell you who you are."[9] Understanding these complexities informs how we analyzed the texts themselves, the different perspectives of the authors, and their interpretations of events.

Two examples illustrate memory dissonance. When Samora and the platoon he led began training in Algeria, there were intense disagreements among the recruits on whether whites and South Asians born in Mozambique should be allowed to participate. On occasion, the debate precipitated conflict between Samora and another guerrilla who vehemently disagreed with Samora's insistence that one did not have to be either black or Mozambican to fight with FRELIMO. Raimundo Pachinuapa, Samora's political ally, described Samora physically subduing his rival. Jacob Jeremias Nyambir, who was also there, insisted that an older guerrilla, Lindoklindolo, intervened to prevent the fight. They not only told different stories, but disagreed about when and where the altercation occurred. Nyambir claimed this was in Algiers, shortly after the FRELIMO recruits arrived from Dar es Salaam. Pachinuapa recalled it taking place somewhat later at Marniah, a remote region near the Algerian-Moroccan border. Pachinuapa's account, collected after the president's death, emphasized Samora's masculinity and physical prowess—an image both Samora and FRELIMO promoted—and thus might have been affected by nostalgia. Nyambir shared his account with us in 2019. While respectful of Samora, he had no reason to embellish the story—but his memory, so many years later, might have been faulty.

The second example is common in contemporary Mozambique. After years of pervasive corruption and rapidly increasing inequality, many citizens longingly look back to the time of Samora's presidency, when social and economic justice were the stated goals of the revolution and corruption was severely punished. In doing so, they often romanticize Samora's leadership, forgetting the difficulties of daily life.

While most writing about Samora focuses on him as a political actor and his public persona, we have expanded our perspective, whenever possible, to include neglected aspects of his personal life. We do so not only to humanize Samora, with all his foibles, flaws, and passions, but also to challenge constructions of his life that separate public from private and political from personal. Too often biographers pay little attention to the personal lives of prominent male political leaders.[10] Historical agents cannot be fully understood, however, without reference to the personal.

Throughout his life Samora struggled to balance his personal and political commitments. His correspondence with his first wife, Josina, whom he lovingly referred to as Jozy, is filled with anguish and a sense of remorse that military responsibilities kept him away from her and their baby Samito for long periods of time. He was particularly concerned about her frail health—with good reason. On August 7, 1971, less than two years after they married, Josina died. Although Samora was devastated, he returned to the battlefield almost immediately after the funeral, leaving his son in the care of his surrogate FRELIMO "family."

Similarly, he was reluctant to remove from their high-ranking positions "old comrades" who had become ineffective or corrupt, because of deep personal bonds or his appreciation of their previous sacrifices. This tendency complicated and contradicted his public persona as a leader who did not tolerate incompetence or corruption.

As researchers, we have the responsibility to reflect, analyze, and access contemporary representations of the past and to raise new questions about Samora's legacy. Hopefully, we will continue to join other scholars in delving into the issues raised here. Samora Machel, and the many other less visible women and men who died in struggles for freedom, left an indelible mark on the continent. Their stories, told from various perspectives, must not be lost to posterity.

1

Living Colonialism

The Making of an Insurgent

Samora Moises Machel was born on September 29, 1933, in the village of Chilembene in Gaza Province, located in the southern part of Mozambique. The son of Mandande Moisés Machel and Guguiye Thema Dzimba, he entered the world as a colonial subject defined by a great number of legal and social restrictions. In Mozambique's racial geography, there were schools he could not attend, hospitals where he could not be admitted, places he could not live, and occupations he could not pursue. Indeed, forces beyond his control regulated much of his early life.

Racism, economic exploitation, and limited possibilities helped shape the formative years of Samora and his age-mates. Most Africans suffered silently, trying to find ways of coping with a harsh world in which survival was a challenge. A handful, like Samora, defied the colonial order. This youthful defiance earned him a reputation as a rebel. As he matured, Samora began to dream of an entirely different world, finding ways to express his opposition to colonial policies and colonialism itself.

Southern Mozambique: The Colonial Context

Although Portugal established a nominal presence along the coast of Mozambique in the late fifteenth century, Lisbon was only able to impose a semblance of control over the southern hinterland in 1895 when its army defeated the Gaza ruler Ngungunyane. Samora's grandfather, Malengani, was a well-known warrior who was seriously wounded fighting alongside Ngungunyane. Tales of Malengani's battle-scarred body and heroism circulated throughout southern Mozambique, and the personal accounts passed down to Samora made him proud of his family's anticolonial past and became part of his political education.

During the early twentieth century the colonial army, consisting largely of African recruits, was with its superior firepower able to overrun other resisting African polities, allowing Lisbon to impose a highly structured authoritarian regime throughout most of the country. Ranked below the colony's governor general were the provincial or district governors (usually military officers), district administrators, and their local counterparts, *chefes de posto.* Each district was divided into European areas, enjoying limited self-government, and non-European ones where residents had few basic human rights. Poorly educated and poorly trained, colonial administrators often ruled as petty tyrants with absolute power to accuse, apprehend, try, and punish their subjects.

The colonial regime similarly depended on African subordinates. Local chiefs (*regulos*), exempt from taxation and forced labor (*chibalo*), became state functionaries empowered to enforce colonial policies, settle minor disputes, and maintain public order. African police (*sipaios*), often recruited from the ranks of colonial soldiers and families of loyalist chiefs, were stationed at every administrative post, where they collected taxes, recruited labor, transmitted the orders of the administrator, and intimidated the local population. Separate legal systems governed "civilized" Europeans and "uncivilized" Africans (*indigenas*), whose lives were profoundly shaped by harsh labor and tax codes and the particular personality and practices of the local administrator.

A miniscule number of educated Africans who adopted a veneer of Portuguese culture were granted *assimilado* status by the state. These were a small number of men and even fewer women of African descent who were gainfully employed, Christian, spoke and wrote Portuguese, and no longer practiced "native customs." Under the authoritarian Salazar regime (1932–68), however, the rights of citizenship meant very little, even for whites. As Raul Honwana emphasizes, noted assimilados were exempted from the forced labor system and offered "a way of seeking a less degrading life for our children," but little else.[1] In 1950, the 4,380 assimilados comprised less than one tenth of 1 percent of the estimated 5.65 million Africans.[2] Although the assimilado community expanded with the colonial reforms around 1960, its numbers remained extremely small.

Because Portugal's own economy was underdeveloped and effectively bankrupt, it lacked the capital to make Mozambique profitable.[3] The only resource readily available for exploitation was the colony's African population. Lisbon turned them into commodities through implementation of the Native Labor Code, which subjected all unemployed African males to forced labor.[4] Whenever the state needed workers to construct roads, lay railroad tracks, install telegraph lines, or dig irrigation ditches, local administrators rounded up peasants. On occasion, administrators provided chibalo laborers to private Portuguese enterprises. The minimal compensation received by workers was rarely enough even to pay local taxes, and their withdrawal from household labor led to food shortages and other suffering. Although women were legally exempt from chibalo, many were not only forced to work but also made to submit sexually to Portuguese and African overseers.[5]

Lisbon also made the colony profitable by renting African workers to labor-starved South African gold mines and, to a much lesser extent, to white farmers and industrialists in neighboring Southern Rhodesia. Beginning in 1897, the Rand National Labour Association, subsequently renamed the Witwatersrand National Labour Association, paid the government a fee for each Mozambican worker. It also set up a deferred payment system under which workers received half their wages when they returned home and Lisbon was paid an equivalent amount in gold.[6] By 1910, approximately eighty thousand Mozambicans—representing from 30 to 50 percent of the able-bodied male population in some districts of Southern Mozambique—were working in the gold mines.[7]

Samora's father, Mandande, and another uncle, Toqouisso Gabriel Machel, like the vast majority of Mozambicans who labored in the South African gold mines, came from Gaza Province.[8] To earn money for his taxes, plows, and other commodities, Mandande spent most of the years between 1912 and 1926 apart from his family.

In 1926, a military coup brought down the Lisbon government. Four years later, António Salazar came to power, ruling Portugal and its colonies for over forty years.[9] Salazar premised his colonial strategy on two broad propositions—that the colonies must remain a permanent part of Portugal to advance its international standing and strengthen its economy, and that Portugal's role was to "civilize" the Africans. To bolster the metropolitan economy, Mozambique was expected "to produce the raw material and sell it to the Mother Country in exchange for manufactured goods," which necessarily required the continued exploitation of cheap African labor.[10] The Salazar regime paid only lip service to its civilizing mission: in 1941 it made the Catholic Church responsible for educating Africans up to the third-grade level, which clearly was insufficient to lead the African from "a savage to a civilized life."[11] The only exceptions were the small number of assimilado children who were allowed to attend European schools.

Medical treatment was also primarily reserved for the settler community in the urban centers. Health facilities in rural areas remained virtually nonexistent. Only a handful of doctors worked in the countryside and the state allocated limited funds for rural health services. Africans' poor diets and the lack of medical facilities and sanitation systems made them highly susceptible to infections and parasitic diseases, such as cholera and smallpox, and diseases caused by malnutrition, such as kwashiorkor.

Life under Colonial Rule

It was into this harsh, uncertain, and often violent world that Samora was born. His first name came from a maternal uncle, Samora Mukhavele, who fought in the Portuguese army during World War I, battling German forces in northern Mozambique, and came back with tales of far-off insurrections there. Samora also reveled in the exploits of his grandfather Malengani and listened intently as his father, mother, and especially his aunt Malungwanya Machel—who was remembered as a "living library"—described in detail the exploits of family members dating back nine generations.[12] Elders also recall that as a boy Samora often rested under a large tree that was a symbol of Gaza resistance, musing on the past.[13] History was clearly one of his early passions.

Singing was another. Samora was brought up in a culture in which music was an integral part of daily life. People sang when they were happy and when they were sad. They sang at births and deaths and other critical moments in the life cycle. They sang while working in the fields and herding cattle. Samora was no exception.

Thanks to the labors and sacrifices of his parents, Samora was born into a relatively prosperous family. Beginning in 1912, his father, like thousands of other young Mozambicans, avoided chibalo by trekking long distances to the South African mines. Dangerous conditions meant that many Mozambicans suffered from rockslides, industrial accidents, contagious diseases, and even death—conditions that adversely impacted the Machel family in many ways. When Samora's eldest brother died in the mines, the mining company sent forty pounds as compensation. Other relatives came home without limbs, blind, or deathly sick from tuberculosis or pleurisy—for which they rarely received even token compensation.[14] Nevertheless, men kept going back and some rural families, including Samora's, whose father worked there for nine eighteen-month periods, became relatively affluent as a result.[15]

Samora never forgot their suffering. Half a century later he spoke of his pain and anger with Allen and António Alves Gomes as they walked along the white sands of Wimbe Beach in Pemba, taking umbrage with those who criticized him for signing the unpopular Nkomati Accord with the apartheid regime. "I have spent my life fighting apartheid and there is not one day that I do not remember the suffering [the South Africans] caused my family and the people of the region."

Samora's mother and thousands of other women were left not only to perform the household labor necessary to sustain the family, but also to chop down trees and clear brush to create the maize and sorghum fields and small vegetable gardens they spent long hours cultivating. Some of these more strenuous tasks had been performed by women even before colonialism because men were often absent for long periods of time, hunting or visiting relatives. After the opening of the mines, Guguiye had to learn how to plow with the draft animals purchased with her husband's wages, despite local taboos that barred women from such tasks.

By 1926, Mandande and his family no longer lived off his wages from the mines. They had become successful farmers, using his four plows and animal traction to cultivate upwards of sixty acres in the rich alluvial soils adjacent to the Limpopo River and selling their agricultural surplus at local and regional markets. By the time Samora was ten, he was working in the family cotton fields and learning how to use a plow. Forty years later, Samora's father proudly told Allen that Samora "worked very hard and was very respectful."[16]

Nevertheless, the family's relative prosperity was precarious. African farmers were forced to sell their produce at artificially depressed prices because colonial administrators fixed prices in ways that privileged European producers. In a 1974 interview, Samora complained that "we would produce and sell one kilo of beans at three and a half escudos while the European farmers produced and sold at five escudos a kilo."[17] European merchants would then resell the beans to Africans for almost double the buying price.

Despite their lack of control over the markets, Mandande and other farmers worked hard and were able to save some of their income, which they reinvested in cattle and agricultural equipment. A handful of prosperous farmers who, like Samora's father, had been schooled at Protestant missions were even recognized as assimilados. Although his family benefited from this relatively privileged status, it never blinded Samora to the suffering of those around him, and he was very critical of those who internalized the colonial civilizing myth and tried to emulate the Portuguese.

Samora was raised in a stern, but loving, home. His deeply religious Protestant parents bestowed upon him the middle name Moises to honor both his father and the biblical figure who led his people out of captivity. A half-century later at the time of his father's death, Samora described him as a "soldier, successful cattle-keeper, innovative farmer, and a moral giant who fought against paganism, against witchcraft and alcohol. But above all else he was like a giant tree whose resolve against colonialism never wavered."[18] Although there is no evidence that Mandande was involved in early nationalist activities, like many of his generation he instilled in Samora a sense of pride in his African past and encouraged his son to think critically about Portuguese rule.

Samora's mother, according to family friends, was a powerful woman in her own right from whom he inherited his self-confidence, defiant attitude, and great pride in his African past.[19] She devoted herself to organizing and maintaining the Compound Mission, a Free Methodist church. When in 1937 Roman Catholic priests, aided by colonial authorities, pressured members of her community to convert to Catholicism, she mobilized fellow church members in opposition.[20] Under her watchful eyes, Samora went to church weekly and listened to pastors preach the virtues of hard work, discipline, education, and righteousness. He continued to espouse these values throughout his life.

We know precious little about Samora's early childhood. Like most prepubescent boys, he spent much of his time herding. While the cattle grazed, he and his agemates engaged in stick boxing (*mugayiso*), wrestling, and fist fighting. To avoid powerful blows to the head, stick boxers had to be dexterous and fast. From these activities Samora developed a passion for martial arts and boxing.[21] His children recalled that he continued to take pride in being a champion stick fighter and insisted that this skill had helped him to think strategically in battle.[22]

Those who knew Samora in his youth remember him in different ways, but all agreed about his strong personality. His classmate and lifetime friend Aurélio Manave described him as "competitive and prone to argue if things were not going in the right direction."[23] His cousin Paulo remembered his early bravery, describing the time a calf was caught by a crocodile after wandering to the river's edge. Alerted by another herder, Samora impulsively jumped in the water and threatened the crocodile by screaming and waving a stick. When the frightened beast released the calf, Samora pulled it out of the water by its tail and treated its wounds. Although this story may be apocryphal, it is still told widely in the region.[24]

Over time, Samora increasingly encountered the harsh colonial world beyond his home. Lisbon's grant to the Catholic Church of a monopoly over the education of virtually all African children meant that, if Samora wanted to be educated, he had to attend the Catholic native school at Uamexinga, five miles from his home. This was a windowless cement structure divided into a handful of classrooms where students spent the mornings receiving rudimentary training, with an emphasis on religious education and physical labor, and the afternoons cultivating cash crops and foodstuffs for the church. Because African students were considered inferior, their teachers regularly failed them. Samora's classmate Aurélio Manave remembered that "on average black students had to attend six years of primary education to complete a three-year course."[25]

It took Samora two years to complete the first grade, after which he was expelled—possibly because of his defiance. Indeed, it was during this period that his classmates began referring to him as "the rebel." Others suggested that the expulsion was due to his Protestant affiliation. Whatever the case, he returned to his family kraal and herded cattle for two years before his father insisted he return to the school. Despite numerous conflicts with his teacher, Samora managed to complete third grade in 1948 at the age of 14.

By the time he enrolled in fourth grade, Samora had become a voracious reader with a passion for learning. He was preparing for his fourth-grade examination when church officials informed him he could only take it if he converted to Catholicism.

When there were just 15 days to go before the 4th grade exam, they told me: either you are baptized, or you leave the mission. It was Father Romano who said so. The Sisters of Charity came to talk to me and they said: either you are baptized or you leave the mission. . . . It was blackmail. I agreed, and I was baptized and christened. They gave me a lot of gifts. Bags with pictures of St. Francis Xavier etc. They were pleased because they had won, they had converted a Protestant. That was in 1950.[26]

Samora was one of only a handful who passed the exam. Two years earlier, only two African students out of more than seven thousand in the region had done so.[27] By then, Samora was dreaming of becoming a doctor, which both the priests and local Portuguese officials deemed outlandish, suggesting instead that he enter a seminary.

As a teenager, Samora defied prevailing social hierarchies and blurred ethnic and racial categories by having a serious romantic relationship with a young *mestiça* (mixed-race) girl from a wealthy trading family. When he informed his parents of his intention to marry her, they strenuously objected—not because of her race but because they had bigger dreams for Samora and feared that her father, who owned several rural shops, would pressure Samora to work in one or serve as his chauffeur instead.[28]

Frustrated by his inability to pursue his dream, in 1951 Samora left Gaza for Lourenço Marques, the capital. Because he lacked proper travel documents, the police detained him and sent him back to Gaza, where he worked briefly as an orderly in Xai-Xai. Upon securing the appropriate documents he returned the next year to Lourenço Marques, where he entered the nursing program at Miguel Bombarda Hospital. Nursing was one of the few relatively high-paying jobs open to Africans.

Although Samora was now living in an urban area, he never forgot the suffering and exploitation of rural Mozambicans that he had previously regularly witnessed. Three types of exploitation stood out. First, in the late 1930s the state imposed a forced cotton regime in southern Mozambique. Women and children were required to spend most of their days from September through May felling trees, cleaning fields, planting, weeding, harvesting, and carrying the cotton to market. For a year's labor many households received less than five dollars, which was insufficient to buy the grain they did not have the time to grow. Those who tried to sneak off to their gardens were beaten and sometimes sexually abused by African police and European overseers.[29]

The hardships associated with the cotton regime left an indelible mark on Samora. Decades later, Herb Shore, an antiapartheid activist, asked Samora what had led him to join FRELIMO. Samora smiled and replied, "Perhaps you might expect me to say I read Lenin and all the other books, but that is not the way it happened. As a boy I went with my father. He was forced to raise cotton, I learned from the way he was cheated when he brought his crop to sell. From my own life I was led to FRELIMO."[30]

The second occurred when the Salazar regime required Africans living in the wetlands adjacent to the Limpopo River to cultivate one to two acres of rice for export. Many of Samora's friends and neighbors were forced into this work and others were compelled to construct and maintain the canals and irrigation systems that sustained rice production on European farms. As with the cotton regime, conscription made it extremely difficult for families to produce sufficient food to meet household needs.[31]

The third—displacement of African farmers from their lands in the Limpopo Valley—began in the early 1950s when the colonial state started recruiting hundreds of farmers in Portugal to resettle there. Under the *colonato* scheme, the colonial administration expropriated sixty thousand acres of fertile land, transferring it to settlers who used dispossessed African conscript labor to work the marshes. Within a decade, virtually all of the lower Limpopo valley had been given to colonatos. The results were as far-reaching as they were disastrous. According to Samora, "All those who were farmers, today their ploughs and tractors are useless. All those who had good houses built of stone were expelled to make way for the settlers and forced to live in one room. Our land was expropriated and designated for settlers. . . . The Africans were put on arid lands that don't produce anything, and the regions handed over to the settlers are irrigated by the River Limpopo."[32]

Samora's initial radicalization was shaped not only by the suffering caused by this exploitation but also by other abuses inflicted by the colonial regime, white settlers, cotton company employees, rural merchants, and missionary teachers. Aurélio Manave, who met Samora shortly after he came to Lourenço Marques, remembered his sense of indignation. "[Samora] complained a lot. He always complained a lot. He complained about real issues and of injustices."[33] Samora, however, was not satisfied only to privately find fault with the colonial system. He was openly critical of colonialism and, although he was forced to register for the colonial army in 1958, he vowed that he would never serve.[34]

Samora's critique of colonialism started long before he arrived in the capital. It grew out of the many hours he sat near a sacred tree in Chilembene, where the famous rebel leader Maguiguane, with whom he closely identified, had organized the 1897 insurgency. Samora brought his mother's spirit of defiance, his father's pride in his African past, and his own understanding of oppression with him to Lourenço Marques where he would meet militant nurses, striking dock workers, and radical students, all struggling to end colonial oppression. It was here that he first encountered Eduardo Mondlane, the Mozambican nationalist who would become the founding President of FRELIMO. It is to this story that we turn next.

The Early Political Education of Samora Machel

The Making of a Freedom Fighter, ca. 1950–63

Samora's political education followed a distinctly different path from that of Kwame Nkrumah, Julius Nyerere, Amilcar Cabral, and his compatriots Eduardo Mondlane and Marcelino dos Santos. Unlike these prominent nationalist leaders who studied at universities abroad and lived in major cosmopolitan centers, Samora had only a limited formal education and spent much of his formative years in rural Gaza.

While his radicalization began in the countryside, in the capital he experienced the full weight of colonialism and was exposed to broader anti-imperialist thinking. As a nursing student he encountered abysmal conditions in the African wards and observed the poor treatment non-whites received. In both the city and his workplace he suffered numerous racial indignities and became keenly aware of the power of the secret police and its informants, who seemed to be everywhere. At the same time, he met young African men and women who also longed to be free and became acquainted with a handful of sympathetic Portuguese, *mestiços*, and

Mozambicans of Goan descent who were organizing clandestine opposition to the Salazar regime. Through these encounters, he became aware of the anticolonial and anti-imperialist struggles going on in Africa and many other Third World countries. Then, in 1962, he met Eduardo Mondlane, who later become the first president of FRELIMO and would remain a source of inspiration throughout Samora's life.[1]

Samora's Career as a Nurse

Nursing was one of the few professions open to Africans, predominantly men, that paid reasonably well—making competition for admission to the nursing programs very intense.[2] This was especially true at Miguel Bombarda Hospital, the colony's largest health center. Most African applicants were children of peasants. All had excelled in school, but, unlike Samora, some—such as António Mondlane and Aurélio Manave—had actually been encouraged by sympathetic missionaries and other Portuguese to pursue careers in medicine. António recalled that, because there were few jobs in Chibuto, he had cautiously raised the subject of becoming a nurse with a local doctor. To his surprise, the physician "not only did not oppose it, but thought it was a good idea and urged me to apply."[3] Aurélio similarly benefited from the support of João Filipe, an engineer who allowed him to work part-time so he could prepare the necessary paperwork the Health Service required.[4] Both men became Samora's colleagues and close friends at the hospital.

The hospital was a highly racialized and regimented institution. Male African students and poorer mestiços were housed in a crowded segregated dormitory adjacent to the psychiatric wards. Disquieting shrieks from this wing often punctuated the students' nighttime studies. The dormitory was divided into rooms, each housing several dozen students who slept on narrow beds arranged in tight rows. They lacked proper ventilation, were hot in summer and cold in winter, and had poor sanitary conditions. Female students resided on the other side of the hospital. European and more prosperous mestiço trainees lived off-campus with their families or in nearby residences.[5] While all students spent upwards of sixty hours a week taking classes and assisting doctors and nurses, there was one program for the more privileged and another for *pretos* (blacks).[6]

Samora quickly earned a reputation as a troublemaker because he refused to be subservient in the classroom. According to one colleague, "he complained a lot and wanted to be respected and did not allow himself to be looked down upon by the European teachers and professors."[7] João Ferreira, a Portuguese drug salesman who frequented the hospital, shared this recollection: "Samora was a person with a strong personality. I believe that Samora was born without any sense of racial inferiority or fear. Samora looked at people as equal and treated them accordingly. On racial matters, anyone who thought that he or she was racially superior to Samora got a rude awakening. Samora confronted anyone who was disrespectful or treated him without dignity."[8]

Samora was no less defiant when responding to the callous indifference of many Portuguese nurses and doctors when they ignored or mistreated patients—which earned him the wrath of some of his professors. "There were several occasions after he criticized the doctors,"

Aurélio Manave recounted, "when they wanted to hit him with an X-ray plate, but he blocked them. He did not hesitate a second. This behavior made some people afraid of him."[9] Years later, Samora reflected on the Europeans' lack of concern for African lives.

> In the hospital were various categories or classes reflecting the social and racial structure of colonial-capitalism, ranging from the white settlers to the "assimilated black" and even to the "native." Here was a total lack of concern for the poor patient, which was manifested in the way the doctor or nurses looked at him, in the absence of hygiene in the wards, in license and indiscipline among the workers. Our people were used in the hospital as guinea pigs for new drugs and certain operations, which if successful could later be applied to the bourgeoisie in the private clinics and consultancies.[10]

Predictably, Samora's behavior angered many of the teachers and nurses who evaluated him. Finding him "stubborn and disrespectful," they punished him by ordering, despite his academic record, that he repeat the second year—during which he graduated at the top of his class.[11]

The nursing program, although similarly hierarchical and racist, was also filled with contradictions. African and European students studied together, worked in close proximity, performed similar tasks, and sometimes socialized outside the hospital. As Manave recalled, "we developed very good relationships . . . even though [white students] never stayed in the dorms."[12]

For Samora and his cohort, the segregated dorms became a free space beyond the gaze of European supervisors and state officials, although they always worried about infiltration by PIDE informants. In hushed voices, students from different parts of the colony shared stories of oppression and humiliation. They pored over South African newspaper accounts of African and Asian leaders agitating for independence, and bolder students even smuggled in political tracts by revolutionaries such as Frantz Fanon and Mao Zedong. They read about the National Liberation Front guerrilla campaigns in Algeria, Gamal Nasser's efforts against the British during the 1956 Suez Crisis, and Ho Chi Minh's military campaign to end French rule in Vietnam. In their beds at night, Samora and his colleagues listened to Voice of America and Radio Moscow. They were particularly excited about Ghana's impending independence under the leadership of Kwame Nkrumah and the growing prospect of freedom in neighboring Tanzania and Zambia.

Samora was often at the center of these conversations, Fellow students remember both his militancy and his insistence that "we only live once, and we cannot continue to accept things as they are."[13] Occasionally, these discussions spilled over into whispering in corners of the cafeteria or in stairwells, beyond the gaze of PIDE informers.

His passion for boxing almost matched his fervor for politics. In his youth he had been taken with stick boxing, wrestling, and other martial arts, but with little time in the hospital for such activities he instead began each day with a rigorous round of exercise punctuated by long intervals of rope skipping. Samora was proud of his trim physique and the discipline required to maintain it. Unlike Nelson Mandela, Samora never fought in the ring—although contemporaries recalled one fight with a fellow student to determine who would be leader of the nursing dormitory.[14] He was, however, a fanatical fan of professional boxing. He read the Brazilian magazine *O cruzeiro* religiously, and on the wall above his bed were photos of famous black pugilists—Joe Louis, Ezzard Charles, Archie Moore, and Jersey Joe Walcott—whose legendary accomplishments he would enumerate to anyone willing to listen. While most of his colleagues preferred soccer, Samora regularly attended bouts or listened to international fights, usually involving South African boxers. His obsession with boxing earned him the nickname "the Manassa Mauler" after his hero, the white prizefighter Jack Dempsey.

Since Samora had no responsibilities on Sundays, he partied most Saturday evenings at African dance halls with either female nursing students or girls from the local secondary schools. He especially loved the Djambo Orchestra, considered the finest African band in Lourenço Marques. A dapper dresser with an infectious smile, Samora had a well-deserved reputation as a lady's man. Graça Simbine, who years later became his wife, remembered him as "a person who took pride in his looks, always very well dressed, always well groomed, and . . . eager to impress."[15]

After graduating, Samora's first assignment was at a small hospital on Inhaca, an island across the bay from Lourenço Marques, where he worked from 1956 to 1959.[16] He quickly improved his knowledge of Ronga, the local language closely related to Shangaan, his mother tongue, so he could communicate more effectively with his patients, primarily fishermen and their families. They suffered mostly from outbreaks of malaria, cholera, and dysentery caused by polluted water and lack of proper sanitation, and from tuberculosis and polio brought back by men from the South African mines. According to his neighbor, David Chiankomo, Samora was very popular because he made after-hours house calls. He studiously avoided discussing sensitive political subjects and tried to stay clear of the local Portuguese administrator. "When he was with us," Chiankomo remembered, "he only spoke about fishing, how the construction of our homes was going, but never politics."[17]

During this period Samora began a serious relationship with Sorita Chiankomo, with whom he had two children—Jucelina and Edelson.[18] Although they never married, he brought his family back to the mainland in 1959, when he returned to attend high school in the evenings while working as a nurse at Miguel Bombarda Hospital during the day.

Racism at the hospital was still rampant. As Samora related, "we discovered the very different treatment [of European and African nurses], the different attitudes toward them and to us. And then, of course, we discovered the different level of wages."[19] For the cash-strapped night student, paying tuition was difficult, especially with the birth of his next two children, Olívia and Ntewane.[20] Nevertheless, Samora saved enough to rent a small wood-framed zinc-paneled house with a corrugated roof in the African neighborhood of Mafalala, where he also treated patients.[21] Compared to many of his neighbors who lived in reed dwellings, his family was relatively privileged.

In 1961, Samora transferred to a night school program run by the Methodists, who reputedly were more sympathetic to Africans than their Catholic counterparts. After completing the program, he applied for an advanced nursing course from which blacks had previously been excluded. While excelling in the written exam, he failed both the practical and the oral ones, even though he was conducting research on malaria at the nation's largest hospital.[22] It is likely that his reputation as a troublemaker prevented him from breaking the color bar.

The long hours Samora spent working, studying, and on his increasing political activity did not diminish his passion for reading, boxing, or music. He also undertook to improve his Portuguese by studying classical Lusophonic literature with Adalberto de Azevedo, a respected Portuguese scholar.[23] Meanwhile, he continued holding court about the world's great boxers and listening to rock and roll, jazz, and local *marrebenta* music.

While living with Sorita and their children, Samora became romantically involved with Irene Buque, a young nurse working at the hospital who shared his anticolonial sentiments.[24] They would soon have a daughter, Ornila. Although a critical political thinker, Samora not only failed to question conventional patriarchal norms but actively and selfishly took advantage of them—as did many other revolutionaries of his time.

The Changing Political Landscape in Mozambique

In the early 1960s, three interconnected developments dramatically transformed the political landscapes of both Mozambique and Africa. First, winds of change were sweeping across the continent. Ghana, Guinea, Algeria, the Congo, and Kenya had gained independence, change was imminent in Malawi and Zambia, and in neighboring Tanzania, Julius Nyerere, its first president, was implementing sweeping economic and social reforms.

Even in the most recalcitrant settler states of southern Africa, Africans were openly contesting injustice. In Southern Rhodesia, nationalists organized the Zimbabwe African Peoples Union, led by Joshua Nkomo, to struggle against Ian Smith's white settler regime. In South Africa, Africans, people of mixed race and Asian descent, and progressive whites were intensifying their nonviolent antiapartheid campaign in the face of harsh and swift state reprisals. After the 1960 Sharpeville massacre, both the Pan-African Congress and African National Congress (ANC) announced plans to use military force to bring down the apartheid regime. The Portuguese colonies were not immune. That same year, nationalists in both Angola and Guinea-Bissau launched military attacks against Portuguese installations.

Second, nationalist activities in neighboring states inspired Mozambicans to step up clandestine anti-Portuguese activity in Lourenço Marques and Beira. The Núcleo dos Estudantes Africanos Secundários de Moçambique (NESAM), founded by Eduardo Mondlane and other educated Africans in the late 1940s, gradually emerged as a significant voice of opposition. With branches across the country, its members celebrated Mozambique's rich and diverse history and spoke out against Lisbon's racial policies. In 1947, after Mondlane was deported from South Africa for protesting against racial discrimination, he had returned to Lourenço Marques, where he became a leading force in NESAM. In the 1950s, NESAM was further radicalized when it attracted younger, more militant adherents, most notably Joaquim Chissano,[25] Armando Guebuza,[26] Filipe Samuel Magaia,[27] Mariano Matsinhe,[28] and Luís Bernardo Honwana,[29] who would all become prominent figures in FRELIMO and close allies of Samora.

Despite being under constant surveillance, NESAM engaged in a variety of subversive activities. In 1961, Magaia and other student activists in Lourenço Marques and Beira, aided by their Portuguese friend João Ferreira, left anti-colonial publications in post offices, public bathrooms, bus stations, and other frequented locations.[30] Members supported striking stevedores at the port of Lourenço Marques, met with teachers opposed to the colonial regime, and held covert political meetings in the shantytowns.[31] They organized clandestine outings to the countryside in order to, as Joaquim Chissano later wrote, "help urban students understand the realities in the countryside and, if possible, be in contact with peasants."[32] NESAM even launched a magazine, *Alvor*, which, although severely censored, subtly addressed many critical issues of the day.

NESAM was not the only critic of Portuguese rule. Around 1960, the leadership of the Associação dos Naturais de Moçambique, a club for Mozambique-born whites, was taken over by antifascist Portuguese, many from families who had fled to Mozambique to escape the tyranny of the Salazar regime. The Associação opened its doors to all races and began to organize night-school classes in African townships, which led to its banning in 1961.[33] There were also a handful of radical whites, including João Ferreira,[34] Jacinto Veloso,[35] Rui Nogar,[36] José Luís Cabaço,[37] and Rui Balthazar,[38] who covertly supported the early nationalist movements and, later, the armed struggle.

NESAM and other internal opponents of colonialism received a big boost when Eduardo Mondlane, by then a United Nations employee based in New York, visited Mozambique in February 1961. Protected by diplomatic immunity, Mondlane, antiapartheid activist and recent PhD, was greeted as a hero. In urban churches and shantytowns and his rural Gaza homeland, he met publicly and on occasion privately with dissidents of all persuasions. Mondlane avoided language that PIDE could use as a pretext to deport him or arrest those with whom he met, but when he returned to New York he wrote a widely circulated condemnation of Portuguese rule aimed at mobilizing international public opinion.

Simultaneously, opposition was intensifying in the Mozambican countryside. In early 1960, Mozambican exiles in Tanzania, members of Tanganyika Mozambique Makonde Union (TMMU), sent militants into northern Mozambique to mobilize rural communities.[39] The result was the first large-scale rural protest, which occurred that June in the northern highlands of Mueda. Thousands of peasants rallied peacefully to complain about the abuses of the forced cotton regime, *chibalo*, and price-gouging at rural shops. Colonial retribution was swift, turning into a bloodbath.[40] In a widely reproduced account, Alberto Chipande, who witnessed the killing, described the events leading up to the massacre.

> The governor invited our leaders into the administrator's office. . . . The governor asked the crowd who wanted to speak. Many wanted to speak, and the governor told them all to stand on one side.
>
> Then without another word he ordered the police to bind the hands of those who had stood on

one side, and the police began beating them. . . . At that moment the troops were still hidden, and the people went up close to the police to stop the arrested persons from being taken away. So the governor called the troops, and when they appeared he told them to open fire. They killed about 600 people.[41]

Although this number, which became part of FRELIMO's revolutionary narrative, was no doubt exaggerated, Honorata Simão Tschussa, a nine-year-old girl at the time, shared with us a similar account: "People surrounded the car transporting prisoners. The Portuguese troops opened fire and massacred them."[42] Cornélio Mandande was even more graphic: "People fell as if they were mangoes during a cyclone."[43]

Third, the role of exiled opponents of Mozambique's colonial regime was changing dramatically. That TMMU members crossed the border from Tanzania to organize protests in Mueda on such a scale was an early indication that the struggle had entered a new phase. Meanwhile, facing the threat of incarceration, hundreds of young men and women from all over the colony, and even some elders, fled to neighboring countries where they joined others already in exile to create organizations committed to overthrowing the colonial regime.

Three distinct opposition groups in exile appeared around 1960. The Mozambican African National Union (MANU), which grew out of TMMU, brought together a cluster of self-help and cultural associations whose members were primarily Makonde.[44] Most were sisal plantation workers in Tanzania and dockworkers in Kenya. In its founding documents, MANU embraced the language of Mozambican nationalism and Pan-

Africanism.[45] Based in Dar es Salaam, it was the largest of the three opposition movements.

The National Democratic Union of Mozambique (UDENAMO) was composed of young dissidents and migrant laborers who came primarily from central and southern Mozambique.[46] Most fled to Southern Rhodesia, which became the center for its activities.[47] Nevertheless, UDENAMO was able to organize secret cells in Lourenço Marques. It later moved headquarters to Dar es Salaam. In 1962, influential opposition figures from the Beira region, most notably Reverend Uria Simango, joined UDENAMO.[48] So did Marcelino dos Santos,[49] a mestiço intellectual who had studied in France, and Helder Martins, a Portuguese doctor.[50]

The National African Union of Independent Mozambique (UNAMI) was the smallest of the three. Headquartered in Blantyre, Malawi, its members came primarily from parts of Tete and Zambézia districts bordering the neighboring British colony. Many had lived there for a long time before joining UNAMI, and its official communiques were primarily in English.

This brief overview reveals the narrow bases of these organizations and the importance of migrant laborers in their membership. Their regionalism and ethnic parochialism posed obvious organizing problems. So did the colony's geographical expanse, which stretched over twelve hundred miles from the Tanzanian to the South African borders. Both factors made forging a broad-based anticolonial coalition a daunting task.

This task fell to Eduardo Mondlane, who was already well-known in anticolonial circles. Shortly after his 1961 visit to Mozambique, he resigned from his

United Nations position and relocated to Dar es Salaam. There, with the help of Tanzanian president Julius Nyerere and the backing of President Kwame Nkrumah of Ghana, Mondlane forged a fragile alliance of these three organizations under the banner of the Frente de Libertação de Moçambique (Front for the Liberation of Mozambique; FRELIMO). The process proved difficult and was never fully realized. After three months of discussion during which the parties tried to hammer out the goals of the movement, some prominent exiles stopped participating. "There was always opposition," recalled Alberto Chipande, who was later selected to lead the initial FRELIMO attack inside Mozambique.[51]

At FRELIMO's First Party Congress in September 1962, Mondlane was elected president, Uria Simango, whom Mondlane defeated, was selected as deputy president, Marcelino dos Santos took charge of external relations, and Joaquim Chissano was appointed Mondlane's personal secretary. Many of the other leaders were either mission-educated Mozambicans from the south whom Mondlane knew personally, or northern Mozambican militants who were primarily Makonde—precipitating charges of favoritism from guerrillas born in the central part of the country. That FRELIMO was a "front" comprised of groups with competing views and agendas underlay its fragility. Looking back, participants agreed that "the early days of FRELIMO were marred by mutual recriminations, expulsion and withdrawal."[52]

Samora's Anticolonial Activity

Samora gradually became involved in nationalist activities. After returning to Lourenço Marques from Inhaca in 1959, he helped organize clandestine meetings of nurses, orderlies, and other workers at the hospital, where he distributed anticolonial material. Because he was a nurse he did not participate in NESAM, but he was in contact with Joaquim Chissano and other militant students. Two years later, he and a fellow nurse, Albino Maheche, met with Mondlane at the home of Mozambican poet João Craveirinha. When PIDE arrested Maheche soon afterward, he refused to implicate Samora in any subversive activities.[53]

From then on, however, Samora was under constant PIDE surveillance, which merely accelerated his flight from Mozambique. For some time, he and two other activists, Thomas Kumalo and Simeão Massango, had been planning to flee to Dar es Salaam so they could join FRELIMO. Samora's long-term goal, however, was to continue his education abroad, and he hoped that FRELIMO would send him to Moscow's Patrice Lumumba University. Father Matias Chicogo of the Anglican Church in Maciene, who had close personal connections with King Sobhuza II of Swaziland, was helping to organize their escape.

Despite being brought up by Christian parents, Samora had not totally rejected the elders' beliefs that ancestor spirits would protect travelers on long and dangerous journeys. Thus, it was not surprising that he and Kumalo consulted a well-known Ronga healer before fleeing abroad. A close confidante of Samora's described the encounter.

> The launch of *tihlolo* [when the healer pulls out
> a basket filled with numerous bones, stones, and
> divining shells] is a moment that fills with anticipation

and anxiety for all those who consult a healer. . . . After he had muttered some imperceptible words, the healer raised his eyes and stared at the two men. "I see you fleeing from this land. But you did not commit any crime. You are scared you will suffer a lot during the journey. But you will arrive. You will not be arrested and this one—pointing the index finger to Samora—I see you coming back again as a great Chief."[54]

In March 1963, while escape plans were crystallizing, João Ferreira, a white anticolonialist activist who had befriended Samora and Irene, learned from his friend Vitório Hugo, an officer in the colonial army, that Samora would soon be detained by PIDE. Ferreira slipped into the infirmary where Samora was working and urged him to escape immediately.[55] Alarmed, Samora and Kumalo took his advice, planning to join up with Massango, who had already left Mozambique.

After securing a holiday leave at the hospital and meeting with underground FRELIMO members who had planned the journeys of other dissidents, Samora informed his family "that he was going abroad to fight [for] Mozambican freedom"—a concept many of them did not fully comprehend.[56] His wife Irene, who only three weeks earlier had given birth to a baby girl, tearfully begged him to stay. Samora, for whom politics trumped family obligations, was unmoved.[57] He quickly arranged for Lomba Viana, a sympathetic Portuguese doctor, to watch over his family and bid Irene farewell.

For the next decade Samora had no contact with his relatives, who paid a heavy price for his commitments. Because of their relationship, his brother Josefate was imprisoned for more than a decade. In 1968, Portuguese security forces burned down his parents' brick home in Chilembene, forcing them to relocate to a crowded thatch-roof hut.[58]

On March 4, Samora and Kumalo took a ferry to Catembe and trekked through Matuituine district, crossing into Swaziland four days later. For Samora, March 8th would always be a day of celebration "marking his freedom from colonialism."[59] By the time PIDE learned of their flight, they were safely in Swaziland. With the help of Reverend Chicogo's son and Swazi officials, they were whisked through the kingdom. After crossing through South Africa, they were arrested at the Southern Rhodesian border. While many compatriots were either incarcerated or died mysteriously after similar detentions, Prince Macucu of the Swazi royal family convinced the Southern Rhodesian police to let the two return to Swaziland, from which they crossed into South Africa and made their way to Botswana, as had other militants before them.[60] In Francistown, Samora and Kumalo contacted members of the Botswana Peoples Party and the exiled ANC. According to Joe Slovo, commander of its military wing, the ANC guerrillas were so impressed by Samora's resolve that they bumped one of their recruits from the flight to Dar es Salaam to make room for him.[61] To Samora's delight, his old friend João Ferreira followed shortly thereafter on a military plane commandeered by Jacinto Veloso, a renegade Portuguese Air Force captain.

3

The Struggle within the Struggle, 1962–70

When Samora arrived in Dar es Salaam in May 1963, FRELIMO was embroiled in an intense internal conflict. FRELIMO's official story, that there were two factions, one "reactionary" and the other "revolutionary," obscures more than it reveals. In reality, the cleavages were multiple, reflecting deep-seated disagreements over race, regionalism, and tribalism and different visions of the appropriate political, economic, and social structure of an independent Mozambique. Personal rivalries and jealousy exacerbated these tensions. In fact, members of the Front agreed about very little other than their desire for independence.[1]

Samora and other new recruits were questioned by Raimundo Pachinuapa, a senior FRELIMO figure and close supporter of Mondlane whose job was to determine if they were spies for the colonial regime. Asked why he had fled Mozambique, Samora did not hesitate in rejecting Pachinuapa's assumption that he had run away, since for him that would have been a cowardly act: "We did not flee, we came here to join FRELIMO."

Pachinuapa also asked each recruit whether he preferred to study or begin military training. This was a sensitive subject, given that many came to Tanzania believing they would receive scholarships to study abroad. Despite Samora's dream of advancing his education by studying in Moscow, he responded without hesitation that he would prefer to get military training first.[2]

When the new recruits met with President Mondlane, he posed the same question. This time, Samora's response was more tentative. Speaking for his compatriots, he said it would be difficult for many to give up their dreams of advanced education and asked Mondlane to give them time to consider their options. That night, he and his roommate decided to commit to the struggle because they worried that a request to be sent abroad "would reinforce the notion that President Mondlane sends young people from the center and the north to military training, while those of us from the south receive schooling."[3] Mondlane, told of Samora's decision, appointed him chief of a seventy-two-man contingent going to Algeria for guerrilla training.[4]

Before the recruits departed, Mondlane met with them to emphasize "Mozambique's rich history and that they were fighting against Portuguese colonial rule, not against whites."[5] Later in the meeting, he elaborated: "There will be a place on our shores for those Portuguese originally from Mozambique who wish to live there. As citizens they will have equal rights in a free Mozambique."[6]

Training in Algeria

The first platoon of FRELIMO recruits, led by Filipe Samuel Magaia, former NESAM activist and FRELIMO military chief of staff, was sent to Algeria for training in 1962. Algeria was a logical place. The Front de

Libération Nationale had substantial guerrilla experience fighting the French a decade earlier and Algeria's president, Ahmed Ben Bella, was an ardent supporter of liberation struggles. Algeria's geographic position also protected it from Portuguese military incursions, and its Mediterranean ports allowed FRELIMO to receive military support from the Socialist Bloc and economic assistance from supporters in Western Europe. Samora's platoon arrived at the end of the following year. That Mondlane and Pachinuapa accompanied the group suggests the importance FRELIMO's leadership was placing on preparation for the struggle.

The training did not start smoothly. After Mondlane gave a pep talk at the staging area and said Algerians would arrive shortly with provisions, he left to meet with local authorities. Not fluent in Arabic, French, or any of the local languages, the recruits could do nothing but wait, which they were forced to do for some days. "We did not leave, no one appeared, no military authorities, we slept there without even having tea. The next morning Mondlane appeared and expressed surprise that we were still there," recalled Pachinuapa. It turned out the wait was due to the Mozambicans' failure to contact appropriate Algerian authorities. From this fiasco Samora learned two important lessons—that you could not go into an area without preparation and that you needed to establish direct links with local communities.[7]

The recruits eventually were taken by truck to the FRELIMO base at Marniah, a desolate site near the Moroccan border lacking even minimal sleeping accommodations. After constructing makeshift barracks and receiving boots and uniforms, the platoon was divided into three sections, each with a group leader. As part of building a common sense of nation, Samora included guerrillas from different regions in each group. For some, this was initially shocking. Jacob Jeremias Nyambir, who was from the south, admitted that his encounter with northern Makonde recruits was jarring. "This was the first time I lived with someone who had facial scarring and lip plates and I was scared. But after a short while we became good friends."[8]

While awaiting their Algerian instructors and supplies, they kept busy performing makeshift tasks—rising early for exercises, working on the barracks, sweeping and cooking. Conversation invariably turned to politics, during which they shared their views and dreams for the future. As instructors and weapons still failed to arrive, these exchanges quickly degenerated into gripe sessions about having to perform domestic chores most considered women's work. Samora responded by example: "He took a rag and began to wipe the floors and tables. Others followed."[9]

Meanwhile, fault lines began to surface. There were complaints about the presence of *assimilados* and *monhé* (a derogatory term for Mozambicans primarily of Goan descent). Some recruits insisted that, because these people were not Africans, neither they nor Mondlane, who considered them Mozambicans, could be trusted. Some, on the other hand, worried they would not be loyal to Mondlane.[10] Others simply objected to the fact that many of these "non-Africans" held positions as nurses, teachers, and group leaders thanks to their greater access to education under the Portuguese colonial regime.

Samora organized mandatory study groups to tackle the divisive issues of race and national identity.

Initial results were mixed. "We scheduled political meetings, and some did not attend. They would say, 'we are not going to those classes, they are tricksters' classes and they are planning how to get rid of Mondlane.' When we were all together as a group, the discussions were heated and sometimes caused indiscipline." During one particularly intense debate, Samora abruptly interrupted, as he was often prone to do. "We are here to train for the armed struggle against Portuguese colonialism. . . . We are not against whites, not against mulattoes. . . . We are not assassins, we want to liberate our country. That is our objective, that and nothing else."[11] Tino Armando, another recruit, vehemently disagreed, insisting that mulattoes and whites were evildoers. Samora became livid, an altercation ensued, and Samora was victorious.[12]

Once the Algerian instructors arrived, there was little time for study groups or political debate. Samora's platoon was sent inland for training. The Algerians, working through translators, pushed its members and the small group of African National Congress fighters training with them day and night.

> It was crazy. It was really crazy. . . . From the moment we awoke we were always on the move. We had fifteen minutes for breakfast. We would carry food to eat while we were training. We would take everything: ammunitions, grenades, and everything. Our bodies would feel heavy. Sometimes we would even put a whole watermelon in our backpacks, but we often did not have [time] to eat it and had to carry it back to camp. Sometimes we would fill canteens with water,

but not have the time to drink it. The instructors would walk while giving lessons and they would arrive at a place and stop there and offer a class. They would run, climb a mountain, and stop at the top of the mountain, they would provide more instruction while running down the mountains. The instructors would come behind us. They would open fire not with fake bullets but with real bullets. The bullets landed around us and the instructors would say, "if you die it is not my fault, I am here to train you." It was very tough training and it was every day. Samora was always there disciplining everybody.[13]

After more than six months of training, Samora and his contingent returned to Tanzania.[14]

Divisions within FRELIMO

Samora was subsequently placed in charge of the military training camp at Kongwa. By 1965, he was commanding FRELIMO's major base at Nachingwea—less than seventy miles from the Mozambican border—which became the staging area for FRELIMO attacks inside Mozambique.

As a senior military leader and one of Mondlane's trusted allies, Samora became embroiled in FRELIMO's internal debates. The leadership's disagreements were ferocious, generating distrust, intrigues, defections, even assassinations. The united front FRELIMO presented to the outside world actually masked two sets of alliances, which themselves disagreed on many issues.

The first centered around President Mondlane and others, including Samora, who embraced the radical and

Figure 3.1. Samora's parents, Moises Mandande Machel and Guguiye Thema Machel. Courtesy of Centro de Documentação Samora Machel (CDSM)

Figure 3.2. Samora exercising. (CDSM)

Figure 3.3. Samora as a nurse. (CDSM)

nonracial platform adopted at the First Party Congress in 1962.[15] The West's support of Portuguese colonialism had driven Mondlane and many of those around him to adopt a more radical anti-imperialist stance, to the consternation of some of his more nationalist followers. This first group was backed by their host President Nyerere of Tanzania, who facilitated Mondlane's meetings with the Organization of African Unity and the socialist countries.[16]

The second faction consisted of discontented nationalists who rejected FRELIMO's new direction.[17] The two most prominent figures were Vice President Uria Simango and Lazaro Nkavandame, a respected Makonde elder who had organized a cotton cooperative in northern Mozambique and helped FRELIMO organize Makonde migrant workers in Tanzania.[18] Mateus Gwenjere, a priest from Sofala who joined FRELIMO in the mid-1960s with a number of his students, also criticized Mondlane's group. Although all three opposed FRELIMO's radical turn and the leadership's punishment of dissidents, they did not speak in one voice. While Simango and Gwenjere adopted an antiwhite stance, Nkavandame did not. Similarly, neither Nkavandame nor Gwenjere flirted with Maoism, which Simango found appealing. Gwenjere was also critical of the leadership for failing to send recruits abroad to study.

FRELIMO's internal conflicts centered around multiple but interrelated questions: What role did race play, if any, in determining who should be considered Mozambican? Who was the enemy? What role should educated Mozambicans have in FRELIMO? What tactics would be most effective in carrying out the armed struggle? What type of postcolonial society did FRE-LIMO envision?

These cleavages further exacerbated preexisting regional and religious animosities. They were also fueled by personal ambition and Lisbon's sustained propaganda campaign focusing on historic tensions between Makua and Makonde and the influence of Marxists within FRELIMO.[19]

Even with this mix of factors, the racial question and the related issue of who was an "authentic Mozambican" was at the center of the conflict. Simango, Nkavandame, and their supporters defined the enemy exclusively in racial terms. For them, all settlers living in Mozambique, including mulattoes and Asians, were either collaborators or simply benefited from Portuguese rule, making them the enemy.[20] They rejected the First Party Congress's antiracialist policy and were livid that Mondlane and his allies welcomed progressive whites, mulattoes, and Asians into FRELIMO. Their vocal opposition violated a cardinal principle of FRELIMO's political culture, that militants had to speak in one voice once consensus had been reached.

The issue of race was brought to a head by the arrival in Dar es Salaam of João Ferreira and Jacinto Veloso, two white Portuguese who came to join FRELIMO.[21] Simango and his supporters were irate, insisting that only black Africans were authentically Mozambican. For both Mondlane, married to a white North American, and dos Santos, pigmentation was subordinate to politics. Matters only worsened with the appearance of Helder Martins, a dissident doctor of Portuguese descent whose services were badly needed by the undertrained FRELIMO medical staff, and Fernando Ganhão, a prominent educator, both of whom had fled Lisbon. Under pressure from Tanzanian security officials, FRELIMO leaders agreed to send the four to Algeria and elsewhere to work with other political exiles.[22] Although there is no indication that Samora opposed this decision, he must have been disappointed, given his position on the issue of race.

The divide over race also influenced FRELIMO's military strategy. Those who viewed all Portuguese as the enemy advocated random attacks on European settlers and urban violence—similar to what had occurred in Algeria. On August 24, 1964, a month before FRELIMO's war announcement and six months before the celebrated attack at Chai in Mueda, a small band led by Lucas Fernandes, a FRELIMO member who had publicly expressed his hatred for whites, killed a Dutch clergyman at the Catholic missionary station in Nangolo, in Cabo Delgado.[23] FRELIMO condemned the murder. Both Mondlane and Samora rejected rash urban violence, which would necessarily kill defenseless men, women, and children and put their supporters at risk.[24]

Mondlane, Samora, and other senior military officers envisioned an alternate strategy focusing on political and military mobilization of exploited peasants. It required FRELIMO guerrillas to forge bonds with local villagers based on shared political goals and peasant involvement in all aspects of the struggle. This position was heavily influenced by the successful anticolonial struggles of the Chinese and North Vietnamese.

Regional cleavages also figured prominently in the bitter dispute over FRELIMO's role in furthering the education of its recruits. Many students who fled to Dar es Salaam in the early years came from rural areas in central and northern Mozambique, where there were limited opportunities to study, and had joined FRE-LIMO hoping they would be sent overseas to advance their education.[25] Few wished to follow Samora's example by going first to the front lines. In 1966, however, FRELIMO's Executive Committee abandoned its policy of sending recruits overseas, fearing the program was creating two tiers of militants—those educated abroad and those forced to fight. The new directive, pushed by Armando Guebuza, FRELIMO's education secretary, also required that those studying abroad or attending the Mozambican Institute in Dar es Salaam undergo months of military and political training at Nachingwea, under Samora's command. Thereafter, they would be assigned duties on the front line, such as working with illiterate peasants in bush schools or constructing make-shift medical facilities.

This did not go over well with many students.[26] By the beginning of 1968, students at the Mozambican In-stitute were in open rebellion. After Samora helped quell the protest, the institute was closed. William Minter, a teacher there, wrote that some who protested were mo-tivated by "the idea that their own personal success and future education [took] priority over the needs of the revolution."[27] Some frustrated students fled to Kenya or the United States and other Western nations, where they helped to form the União Nacional dos Estudantes Moçambicanos to oppose FRELIMO policies. Although not terribly successful, UNEMO did publish a bitter attack on Mondlane, claiming that he forced them to interrupt their educations to maintain his position as the only FRELIMO member with a PhD.[28]

The two factions also held very different visions of an independent Mozambique. Simango and Nkavandame adopted a nationalist position under which an educated black elite would rule, as Malawi and Kenya were governed. Samora sided with Mondlane and the FRELIMO Executive Committee in condemning this elitist approach, which, they argued, would lead Mozambique toward a neocolonial arrangement common in other African countries. Instead, they imagined a society free of racial, social, and economic inequality, responsive to the needs of peasants and workers, that would attack poverty and underdevelopment through the transforming capacity of education, science, and technology.[29]

In 1968, Mondlane acknowledged that FRELIMO was moving in a socialist direction, the first time any FRELIMO leader had made a public reference to Marxism. Several years earlier, however, Samora was already contemplating a more radical trajectory. Among his personal papers, we discovered a tattered field notebook written either in late 1966 or early 1967. After asking himself whether FRELIMO should be a united front or a single party, he listed twenty-two social and political objectives, all of which were later incorporated into FRELIMO's revolutionary ideology. Among the most significant were:

- Support the masses
- Armed struggle within the country
- Unity of all comrades
- Establishment of liberated zones based on people's power

- Down with racism and tribalism
- Avoid revolutionary slogans
- Social justice[30]

Samora's Ascension to Power

As Samora became an increasingly influential advocate of the socialist line, opponents argued that he had been brainwashed by Marxist intellectuals who had hijacked FRELIMO. They pointed to his close relationship with Marcelino dos Santos, Jorge Rebelo, Oscar Monteiro, and Sérgio Vieira, who they insisted were not authentic Mozambicans because of their Goan descent. Implicit in their claims was the elitist assumption that Samora's peasant background and limited education made him incapable of comprehending the complexities of Marxism.[31]

Samora's rivals, however, completely misread the roots of his radicalism, which stretched as far back as his youth. Later, in Lourenço Marques, he experienced discrimination in his workplace, was denied access to segregated theaters, was prevented from moving freely through the city at night, and could be arrested and beaten on the slightest pretext.[32] During this period he also began to question the limited success of African nationalist movements, to recognize the broader achievements of the revolutions in Vietnam and Cuba, and to become aware of how international entities were responding to FRELIMO's anticolonial struggle. In Dar es Salaam, he observed first-hand how China, Vietnam, and Eastern Bloc nations provided FRELIMO military and diplomatic support, while the West turned a deaf ear to its requests for assistance and continued to support Portugal. Samora later described his political development this way: "During the liberation struggle somebody gave me a copy of a book by Marx. I read it, and I realized I was 'reading' Marx for the second time."[33] As one FRELIMO leader explained, "Samora's Marxism came from his gut."[34]

Under Mondlane's tutelage, Samora quickly rose through the ranks. In 1966, FRELIMO's Central Committee appointed him defense secretary to replace Filipe Samuel Magaia, who had been killed on patrol by a dissident FRELIMO member.[35] The decision to select Samora over Casal Ribeiro, Magaia's second-in-command from central Mozambique, fueled suspicions that a southern clique was consolidating power. Samora embraced his new responsibility for planning and coordinating FRELIMO's military campaigns and building a military force and command structure committed to the leadership's radical vision. During the 1968 Second Party Congress, Mondlane would single out Samora for his extraordinary accomplishments.

Meanwhile, PIDE, which had infiltrated FRELIMO, fanned the flames of discord. Its operatives spread rumors ranging from claims of a Marxist takeover to allegations that Mondlane and his wife Janet were CIA agents. PIDE surreptitiously bought off key militants and unleashed a formidable propaganda campaign aimed at exacerbating ethnic and regional tensions by telling members from the center and north that southerners, including Mondlane and Machel, had captured FRELIMO and were promoting friends and family.

The biggest challenge to Mondlane and Samora, however, came from within the FRELIMO leadership.

As the power and influence of the dissidents slipped, they became more outspoken. Simango insisted whites and Asians were corrupting FRELIMO's leaders and that he would not hand over power to "Marxists from the South." Nkavandame opposed the radical turn and, through his ties to senior figures in the Tanzanian government, tried to drive a wedge between Nyerere and the FRELIMO leadership.[36] Gwenjere encouraged alienated students to ransack the FRELIMO office in Dar es Salaam, during which event Central Committee member Matheus Sansão Muthemba was murdered.

On the morning of February 3, 1969, Mondlane was assassinated. As recounted in *Mozambique Revolution*, "on that day, early in the morning, our President went to the office and worked with several comrades. At about 10 a.m. he collected all his mail from the office and went to the home of a friend [an American, Betty King], a quiet place to work undisturbed. Among the mail he took with him was a book, wrapped and addressed to him. Once at the house he started opening his mail. When he opened the book, there was a great explosion, killing our President."[37]

The Portuguese police, probably with the help of a hit man named Cassimo Monteiro, had orchestrated the killing. Although no Mozambicans were charged, PIDE appears to have had accomplices inside FRELIMO who arranged to have the package delivered directly to Mondlane. The two primary suspects were Silveiro Nungu, administrative secretary at the FRELIMO office in Dar es Salaam, and Lazaro Nkavandame.[38]

Mondlane's death precipitated an intense power struggle. In a preemptive move, immediately after the funeral Simango declared himself president. However, his public differences with Mondlane, narrow race-based perspective, and lack of battlefield experience caused many in the leadership to object. At an emergency meeting of the Central Committee weeks later, Simango failed to win a majority, but in an unsuccessful effort to paper over the conflict the Central Committee approved a troika of three coequal presidents: Samora, the military commander; dos Santos, secretary for foreign affairs; and Vice President Simango.

In response, Simango wrote "The Gloomy Situation in FRELIMO," a blistering attack on the other two leaders, in which he claimed that his opponents had usurped power, eliminated political rivals, and planned to kill him. He also condemned Mondlane, arguing that he had fostered the growth of a new form of colonialism in FRELIMO by allowing Portuguese to dominate the institute, brainwash students, and infiltrate the Central Committee. Simango denied that he and his supporters were racists and insisted they were defending the people's interests by vigilantly preventing imperialists from infiltrating FRELIMO.[39] He also decried the leadership's political violence within FRELIMO and claimed that Samora had personally masterminded the killing of his predecessor, Felipe Samuel Magaia.

Two months later, the Central Committee expelled Simango from FRELIMO and selected Samora to fill the leadership vacuum.[40] He was chosen because of his ties to Mondlane, skills as a military commander, popularity among the guerrillas, and ability to win over rural communities in northern Mozambique. Simango escaped to Cairo and subsequently joined the Comité

Revolucionário de Moçambique, a nationalist organization based in Zambia.[41] Some suspected he was involved in Mondlane's assassination, an accusation that has never been proven.

At roughly the same time, Nkavandame, who had been charged with corruption and exploiting peasants in northern Mozambique, deserted to the Portuguese along with his supporters and urged other Makonde to put down their arms. The colonial regime used his defection to try to win over Makonde communities, but unsuccessfully. This failure was significant because Cabo Delgado had by then become a principal terrain of struggle and an important route used by FRELIMO guerrillas to extend their campaign into Niassa and more southern provinces.

Samora and the Armed Struggle, 1964–75

While the FRELIMO leadership was embroiled in conflict, it was also preparing its guerrillas to confront
Mozambique's colonial army and facing the difficult
task of winning support in rural communities that knew
little about the liberation movement. Samora played a
decisive role in dealing with both these challenges.

Preparing for Armed Struggle

When Samora's platoon returned from Algeria, it was
initially stationed at the FRELIMO camp in Bagamoyo,
Tanzania. Worried the camp would be an easy target for
Portuguese spies, given its proximity to Dar es Salaam,
and that family members living in Dar might distract
guerrillas, FRELIMO moved it to Kongwa in central
Tanzania and appointed Samora its commander.

Conditions at Kongwa, site of an abandoned
groundnut scheme with only three shacks, were even
worse than those in Algeria. The soldiers had only what
they brought with them—blankets, some provisions, and
personal belongings, but no weapons. As Pachinuapa recalled, "[on the] very first day we needed to eat. So, the
question arose who would actually do the cooking. We

considered ourselves well-trained soldiers because we had completed the military course [in Algeria]. Nobody was interested in working in the kitchen. We were fighters not cooks. Samora volunteered. He set the example."[1]

Samora insisted the camp become self-sufficient as quickly as possible. He divided his hundred soldiers into two groups, each spending part of the day working in the fields and building barracks and latrines while the rest engaged in training. Lacking weapons, they simulated combat with sticks until the first cache of light arms arrived from Algeria. Later, they received training with weapons provided by China and Eastern Bloc countries. They learned first aid, how to organize ambushes, and where to plant land mines. During the evenings they engaged in political education and attended literacy classes. According to Chipande, officers and foot soldiers were expected to train side-by-side, work together in the fields, and prepare meals together. This regimen was introduced by Samora to foster recognition that, no matter where in the colony they were born, their survival now depended on supporting each other.[2]

In 1965, FRELIMO moved its major training base closer to the border. It was now at Nachingwea, on an abandoned plantation located less than seventy miles from Cabo Delgado, where FRELIMO had launched its first military actions the year before. Aided by a contingent of Chinese instructors, Samora oversaw the training of more than two thousand male and female guerrillas. With its schools, clinic, collective fields, and women's brigade, Nachingwea was a microcosm of FRELIMO's imagined new Mozambican society. Years later, Samora described it as the "laboratory and forge" of the new nation.[3]

As part of the militants' political education, Samora and the leadership stressed FRELIMO's revolutionary values, demanding the guerrillas shed decadent habits inherited from colonialism and the "obscurantist" beliefs they had learned as children. Helder Martins, who trained nurses at Nachingwea, described the profound influence of the Chinese advisers on Samora's thinking: "They were not only military instructors; they were also political instructors. They suggested readings for Samora, including *The Complete Works of Mao Zedong*, which stressed collectivism, self-discipline, and solidarity with the peasantry."[4]

Samora also sought to create a sense of national identity by instituting cultural activities—dance, song, and theater—from various parts of the colony. On most Saturday nights militants could be found engaging in these activities, which were a welcome break from military and political training. According to Oscar Monteiro, who taught at Nachingwea, these social nights helped to reinforce bonding among the comrades.[5]

Life at Nachingwea was demanding. Work in the fields, military training, and political education consumed all day and much of the evenings. Living conditions were harsh and supplies scarce. Some trainees became dispirited; others abandoned the movement.[6] Another vexing problem was the large number of female recruits who became pregnant during training—and the challenge of supporting these young unwed mothers and their children.[7] Given the leadership's gender biases, it isn't surprising that childcare was left to the mothers and members of the Women's Detachment, who took on the role of "aunties." This sexist behavior notwithstanding, the "lessons of Nachingwea" were an important part of FRELIMO's idealized revolutionary discourse.[8]

Samora could be a severe taskmaster, but he was also sensitive to the difficulties recruits had in adjusting to the demands of life at Nachingwea. On one occasion, he met with a rebellious student from the Mozambican Institute who had been sent to Nachingwea. The student expected to be severely punished. Instead, Samora listened to his grievances, complaints of homesickness, and frustration at not being allowed to train as an artilleryman, which had always been his dream. The following day he was transferred to an artillery unit being trained by the Chinese and became part of the first artillery brigade to fight inside Mozambique.[9]

Guerrilla penetration into northern Mozambique began in 1964. The first front was opened in Cabo Delgado with a sustained incursion into the Makonde highlands led by Alberto Chipande. In November 1965, FRELIMO opened a second front in eastern Niassa. After marching for eleven days and avoiding at least one Portuguese ambush, the small expeditionary force led by Samora arrived at the village of the senior Yao chief, Mataka V. According to some accounts, Samora's group, dressed in Muslim garb to avoid suspicion, met surreptitiously with Mataka and convinced him and his subjects to relocate by following the guerrillas to an area beyond the control of colonial authorities.[10] Years later, António Eanes, president of Portugal, who had been a captain in the colonial army, presented a fuller account of this maneuver at a state dinner—explaining that Mataka was under arrest at a Portuguese administrative center when Samora, dressed as a Muslim holy man, entered the post and whisked him away. Samora, not known for his modesty, grinned and willingly added details. With Mataka free, some of his followers joined FRELIMO in Tanzania. Others who had relocated provided food and logistical support to insurgents passing southward through the Niassa corridor.[11]

This episode clearly demonstrates that Samora understood the important role traditional African leaders could play in the liberation struggle. Mataka's ancestors, like Samora's, had fought against the Portuguese occupation. These living memories nurtured a tradition of resistance, which helps explain why Mataka's Yao followers supported the guerrillas, while other African polities in Niassa that had not resisted were more ambivalent. Years later, Samora appealed to a similar tradition of resistance to mobilize rural supporters in the Zambezi Valley, where anticolonial opposition had persisted until 1921.[12]

By the end of 1965, FRELIMO, having made important inroads in Cabo Delgado and Niassa, opened a front in Tete. While Samora was involved in planning the strategy, he did not personally direct the military campaign. This effort was abandoned months later when it became clear that FRELIMO forces were overextended elsewhere. It was not until 1969 that FRELIMO again challenged Portuguese forces in the Tete region.

Implementing Strategies to Carry Out the Armed Struggle

In pursuing the armed struggle inside Mozambique, FRELIMO had to develop strategies to deal with the challenges that arose. While much has been written on this subject, we will focus on the four most significant challenges Samora faced as military commander.

The first was the guerrillas' relative weakness. FRE-LIMO had barely 250 men under arms, whose weapons were limited to handguns, outdated rifles, light machine guns, and land mines. In his reports from the front lines, Samora complained that lack of arms and ammunition was impeding guerrilla advances both in Cabo Delgado and Niassa.[13] The colonial force numbered more than thirty thousand and had modern weapons, commu-nications equipment, helicopters, jets, and napalm, all provided by Lisbon's NATO allies. Given this imbalance of power, Samora and his comrades calculated it would take twenty years or more to liberate Mozambique.[14]

The second challenge was that, in order to compen-sate for this enormous imbalance, Samora had to recruit large numbers of sympathizers. FRELIMO's leadership had become convinced that Mao's model of protracted guerrilla warfare, with its emphasis on political mobiliza-tion of the peasantry and socioeconomic transformation of the countryside, was the best strategy for liberat-ing Mozambique. Borrowing from the Maoist maxim, Samora and his commanders stressed that "the people are to the guerrillas as water is to fish. Out of the water a fish cannot live. Without the people, that is to say, without the support of the people, the guerrillas cannot survive."[15] To gain this needed support, FRELIMO militants organized meetings in rural communities to explain the objectives of the struggle and grapple with the immediate problems the peasants faced.[16] Samora also used these occasions to establish personal bonds with members of these commu-nities, some of which lasted a lifetime.

In the war zones of Cabo Delgado and Niassa, sympathetic rural communities surreptitiously provided critical foodstuffs and carried war materiel to the front lines from FRELIMO's bases. Maintaining the supply lines was an arduous process and extremely dangerous for the carriers.[17] FRELIMO also deployed younger children to carry messages, since they were less likely to be noticed by Portuguese troops.

Recruiting supporters was challenging. Fear of retribution deterred many peasants from assisting the guerrillas or joining their ranks. Sometimes, FRELIMO forces attacked communities loyal to the Portuguese and coerced members into becoming part of the armed struggle.[18] According to Thomas Henriksen, a historian often critical of FRELIMO, evidence suggests that "the colonial forces were more guilty of indiscriminate killing and mass murder," while FRELIMO engaged "in selective violence and abductions."[19]

The third challenge was effectively incorporating women in all aspects of the struggle. FRELIMO's thin ranks and urgent need to continue expanding its support in the countryside required more cadres. Women were the obvious choice. The Liga Feminina Moçambicana (Mozambican Women's League) was founded in 1966. Its function was to recruit women to transport supplies, provide information about Portuguese military activity, and even carry out small acts of sabotage. They were not, however, seen as potential guerrilla fighters.

Some women, dissatisfied with such constraints, requested military training. The following year, FRELIMO established the Destacamento Feminino (Women's Detachment) under female commanders who had trained at Nachingwea. After training, brigades were dispatched to Mozambique to mobilize peasant women and carry out limited guerrilla activities. The participation of Mozambican women in military campaigns stimulated the gradual restructuring of gender roles within FRELIMO.

One of the first women to be trained was Josina Muthemba, who was born in Inhambane to a rural family with deep nationalist roots. An active member of NESAM and clandestine member of a FRELIMO cell in the capital, she tried in 1964 to flee to Tanzania to join the liberation movement. Rhodesian security forces arrested her and, as was standard practice, handed her over to PIDE. Despite then being under state surveillance, she managed to escape with several other FRELIMO supporters, arriving in Dar es Salaam the following year. For a time, Josina assisted Janet Mondlane, wife of the FRELIMO leader, at the Mozambican Institute. She was later sent to Mozambique to work with orphans and young mothers, organizing day-care centers and securing food, blankets, clothing, and medical supplies. In 1967, she and twenty-four other women were the first to volunteer for military training at Nachingwea, after which she became a leader of the Destacamento Feminino.[20]

Josina's dedication to FRELIMO attracted the attention of Eduardo Mondlane and other senior leaders, including Samora. He was drawn to the energetic and beautiful young militant who had turned down a scholarship to study in Sweden in favor of participating in the struggle. Above all else, he admired Josina's independence of mind and commitment to the revolution. In a letter dated October 22, 1970, he wrote to her that it "brings me joy to know your great capabilities, and how effective you are in the struggle for liberation and particularly in the struggle for Mozambican women."[21]

Despite having a wife and family in Lourenço Marques, Samora openly courted Josina. Shortly thereafter, with FRELIMO's approval, they were married at the FRELIMO Education Center in Tunduru on May 4, 1969—three months after Mondlane's assassination. In a gesture of solidarity, the Reverend Uria Simango, FRELIMO vice president and Samora's principal rival, officiated at the wedding, with many senior FRELIMO and Tanzanian officials attending, including President Nyerere. That November, Josina gave birth to a chubby baby boy they named Samora Jr. but called Samito—"little Samora."

Josina and other female militants pushed FRELIMO leaders to confront a number of issues adversely affecting young women. They lobbied to abolish female circumcision rites and to increase support for pregnant militants. In both regards they were successful. A 1972 FRELIMO commission conducted a study in the liberated zones of the effects of circumcision rites on Makua and Makonde girls and boys. The following year, despite opposition from traditionalists, they recommended eradicating the practice.[22]

His war experiences, pragmatic considerations, and relationship with Josina altered Samora's thinking on gender equality. On several occasions he apologized for his irresponsible and inappropriate behavior toward women, and, despite opposition from more conservative members of FRELIMO, celebrated their importance in the armed struggle. In his much-cited keynote address to the first conference of the Organization of Mozambican Women in 1973, Samora proclaimed:

> The emancipation of women is not an act of charity, the result of a humanitarian or compassionate attitude. The liberation of women is a fundamental necessity for the Revolution, the guarantee of its continuity and the precondition for its victory. The main objective of the Revolution is to destroy the system of exploitation and build a new society which releases the potentialities of human beings, reconciling them with labour and with nature. This is the context within which the question of women's emancipation arises. . . .
>
> If it is to be victorious, the Revolution must eliminate the whole system of exploitation and oppression, liberating *all* the exploited and oppressed.[23]

Note, however, that his thinking had not sufficiently evolved to include gender oppression in the household and the community.

The last challenge was to move beyond the racialized notion held by many of the militants that all Portuguese were necessarily the enemy. Samora refused to accept this and did not allow his forces to commit random acts of violence against European settlers and their descendants.[24] In some areas, commanders even courted European missionaries and sympathetic Portuguese settlers. Samora developed a close personal relationship with Manuel Braz da Costa, a Portuguese farmer in Niassa who provided supplies and information about the movement of colonial forces.[25]

It was also forbidden to abuse Portuguese prisoners of war.[26] This stood in sharp contrast to the well-documented and widespread torture of FRELIMO captives and sympathizers carried out by the Portuguese. In FRELIMO publications, speeches, discussions, and meetings with foreign journalists, Samora regularly highlighted FRELIMO's humane treatment of captured Portuguese soldiers—which proved to be excellent propaganda, challenging Lisbon's claim that the insurgents were little more than "black terrorists." FRELIMO won praise from Western European and North American activists who organized anticolonial protests in African American communities, progressive churches, universities, and labor halls.[27]

Overcoming these four challenges enabled FRELIMO to slowly advance into northern Mozambique. Once it eliminated the Portuguese presence from these areas, dismantling the colonial administration, it had to establish new revolutionary structures, which became the basis for the liberated zones.

The Liberated Zones and *Aldeamentos*: A Terrain of Struggle

The vast, sparsely populated regions of northern Mozambique were the principal terrains of struggle between the guerrillas and the Portuguese regime. Both sides prioritized reorganizing rural society and "protecting" communities under their control, although their strategies were very different. For the FRELIMO leadership, liberated zones brought opportunity to begin to transform social and economic relationships in the countryside. For colonial planners, the goal was to relocate hundreds of thousands of peasants into strategic hamlets to isolate FRELIMO guerrillas from their peasant base of support, depriving them of foodstuff, intelligence and new recruits.

Samora's dual challenge was to create new structural relationships with peasant communities in liberated areas, and to relocate peasants who fled either as individuals or as communities from areas still under Portuguese oppression. Where the guerrillas had replaced the colonial regime, primarily in the northern parts of Cabo Delgado, Niassa, and Tete, FRELIMO established liberated zones. As Teresa Raica, who came from Maua district in Niassa, understood it, FRELIMO's goal was to win hearts and minds and recruit younger people for the struggle by any means possible.

> At first, I was sent to the Gungunhana base and worked as a cook. Then I reached a certain age when I trained at the Mswisisi base. I was with men and other women. We were all together regardless of our ethnic backgrounds. Each spoke her own language. There were no old people. Most were in their 20's. We grew cassava, sorghum and vegetables in the field belonging to the cooperative. I was happy with my life because I chose it. Those who were forcibly recruited did not try to escape because many of them began to warm towards FRELIMO's political views after attending meetings and training. I always said to the people who were captured and brought to the base: "This is for your own good. This is for us to be free. We have to kick out the whites. Let's fight together so that we can

> live wherever we want." People at the base always said
> that unity meant to free ourselves. Socialism? I don't
> know about that.[28]

This persistent belief that the goal was to "kick out the whites" suggests that, like Raica, many peasants in the liberated zones, even after attending political education sessions, had only a superficial understanding of the FRELIMO ideology.

FRELIMO used regularly scheduled meetings to engage the peasantry, giving voice to villagers' concerns and raising their political consciousness. There was nothing Samora valued more than feeling connected to the people, even if these encounters stretched well into the night or early morning. At the end of every meeting, he would urge his listeners to replace loyalist chiefs with popularly elected leaders who would preside over local meetings, establish guidelines for behavior, and organize collective production.

Education as a means to combat illiteracy and superstition was central to Samora's vision of how best to develop popular democracy, and he vigorously promoted educational programs in the liberated zones.[29] Working with the local population, FRELIMO teachers created an embryonic educational infrastructure where few, if any, schools had previously existed. By 1966, more than ten thousand students were said to be attending primary school—a number that tripled over the next four years. Even more adults attended literacy classes, which were seriously overcrowded and lacked enough of both primers and teachers.[30] This was many Mozambicans' first opportunity to learn to read and write—and to be exposed to FRELIMO's revolutionary ideology.

On several occasions, Samora told the story of a captured Portuguese soldier who, to the amazement of FRELIMO guerrillas, could neither write his name nor read. When the prisoner was given a pen and paper he "simply drew lines and stripes, there were no letters, no alphabets. We were trying to figure out if it was Arabic, Asian, Indian, or Chinese. . . . So we asked him to read for us and he responded that he did not know how."[31] The story was instructive both because it underscored the limited educational opportunities available to poor rural Portuguese, and because it challenged the commonly held belief among his own illiterate soldiers and peasants in the Europeans' superiority.

Despite the acute shortage of African doctors, nurses, and other health workers, Samora and his comrades were able to introduce a rudimentary health-care system in the liberated zones.[32] It necessarily emphasized preventative medicine. FRELIMO reported that in 1966 it vaccinated more than a hundred thousand peasants in Cabo Delgado against smallpox.[33]

The colonial agricultural system privileged cotton production for the metropole over family farming and caused recurring food shortages and famines.[34] FRELIMO instead emphasized collective production of basic staples for families and FRELIMO militants. In parts of Cabo Delgado, peasants worked the land jointly and shared produce and profits equally. In other areas they retained control over their own plots but worked collectively several days each month in a communal field growing food for the military. Because Samora believed collective labor helped cement the unity between fighters and local populations, guerrillas on occasion joined peasants in cultivating the communal fields.[35]

For all the benefits of being in liberated zones, conditions were harsh and precarious. There were threats of Portuguese attacks, shortages, intense political education sessions, long working days, and FRELIMO's military discipline, which was very different from how the peasants had previously lived their lives. Some peasants fled, alone or with disillusioned chiefs, while others were seduced by Portuguese promises of food, clothing, and amnesty.[36]

Nevertheless, life in the liberated zones was appreciably better than what most Mozambicans experienced when compelled to relocate to Portuguese strategic hamlets (*aldeamentos*), euphemistically known as "protected villages."[37] The forced relocation of dispersed communities and the colonial state's designation of the vast emptied areas as "free-fire zones" where the military could shoot moving targets on sight intensified resentment of the Portuguese.[38] Government officials estimated that by 1973, fully 67 percent of the African population of Niassa and almost half that of Cabo Delgado had been moved from their historic homelands into aldeamentos.[39] As the war heated up, forced evictions became hastier and more chaotic as entire communities were shoved off their land at a moment's notice, in some cases before any housing was in place.[40] During an unusually frank conversation with Australian journalists, a Portuguese military commander boasted that coercion had no limits: "We give the blacks two weeks to come into fortified villages. If they don't, we shoot them."[41]

Figure 4.1. Samora and Eduardo Mondlane. Courtesy of Centro de Documentção e Formação Fotográfica (CDFF)

Figure 4.2. FRELIMO's first president, Eduardo Mondlane. (CDFF)

Figure 4.3. Samora instructing members of FRELIMO's Women's Detachment. Courtesy of Centro de Documentação Samora Machel. (CDSM)

Figure 4.4. FRELIMO guerrillas training. (CDSM)

Figure 4.5. Samora addresses soldiers during the armed struggle. Courtesy of António Alves Gomes

Figure 4.6. Josina Machel. (CDSM)

Figure 4.7. Samora and Joaquim Chissano with FRELIMO guerrillas. (CDSM)

Figure 4.8. A woman from the liberated zones offering a papaya to Samora. (CDSM)

The Cost of the War

The conflict was shifting in FRELIMO's favor.[42] In 1970, its forces had withstood a major Portuguese air and ground counteroffensive known as Gordian's Knot. By 1973, several thousand guerrillas were fighting inside Mozambique. In 1974, FRELIMO forces were able for the first time to cross the Zambezi River and open new fronts in Manica and Sofala in the colony's strategic heartland. Lisbon's position was further undermined by increasing international pressure, sparked by the 1972 massacre of four hundred villagers at Wiriyamu in Manica Province.[43] With no end in sight, the Portuguese officers who had overthrown the fascist Portuguese government on April 15, 1974, began negotiating with FRELIMO to end the war.

Nevertheless, it would be a mistake to assume that FRELIMO had won the war or even that victory was near. Claims of the inevitability of such an outcome—which became part of the patriotic narrative after independence—obscure the difficulties on the ground. The guerrillas had suffered heavy losses of both men and materiel.[44] The war had taken the lives of prominent leaders, including Eduardo Mondlane, Filipe Samuel Magaia, and Samuel Kankhomba, and others like Uria Simango and Lazaro Nkavandame had defected.

Samora suffered the loss of many comrades, but most notably Eduardo Mondlane, his mentor and hero. Alberto Chipande, who broke the news to Samora at Nachingwea, remembers him "[falling] to the ground when I told him. I had never seen him crying. He bawled."[45]

The struggle was also difficult for Samora and Josina. Shortly after their marriage, Samora returned to the battlefield. He wrote regularly, describing his pride in all Josina had accomplished, bemoaning the fact that he was gone from her and their child for such long periods, and acknowledging that his absence had complicated her life.[46] His letters expressed deep love for her, as did the parting salutation—"I kiss you passionately Joze"—with which he always ended. Samora was especially concerned about Josina's poor health and urged her not to let the burdens of the struggle wear her down. She persisted in working with war orphans and single mothers, however, even after contracting leukemia.

On April 7, 1971, Josina, his bride of only two years, died at the age of twenty-six. The depth of Samora's pain is expressed in the poem he wrote as a eulogy to his wife and lover, which also reveals how revolutionary discourse permeated personal expressions of grief:

> Josina you are not dead because we have assumed
>   your responsibilities and they live with us.
> You have not died, for the causes you championed
>   were inherited by us in their entirety.
> You have gone from us, but the weapon and rucksack
>   that you left, your tools of war, are part of my
>   burden.
>   . . . .
> The Revolution renews itself from its best and most
>   beloved children.
> This is the meaning of your sacrifice: it will be a
>   living example to be followed.
> My joy is that as patriot and woman you died doubly
>   free in this time when new power and the new
>   woman are emerging.[47]

Samora also faced long periods of separation from his son. Almost immediately after Josina's funeral, Samora returned to the battlefield, leaving Samito at

Nachingwea in the custody of FRELIMO "aunties."[48] The care they provided offers a glimpse into the political kinship of the FRELIMO "family" and the female social networks that enabled men to go to war. A few times a year, Samora would return to Nachingwea to spend time with Samito. Despite having only vague memories of his father, Samito fondly recalled how they frolicked on the beaches near Dar es Salaam, swam in the Indian Ocean, visited the game reserve at Arusha, and even flew to Zanzibar.[49] For Samora, who had no contact with his five children in southern Mozambique, Samito was a precious reminder of everything for which he was fighting.

In the bush without his family and immediate friends, Samora spent most of his time devising military strategies and putting them into practice. When not engaged in battle, he read, wrote poetry, doodled, and followed a daily exercise regimen to maintain his physical fitness. He was also an inveterate list-maker, which was hardly surprising given his very structured and disciplined personality.

The Lusaka Accord and Its Aftermath

The Portuguese coup by the Armed Forces Movement was led by dissident junior officers opposed to continuing the colonial wars. After overthrowing Salazar's handpicked successor, Marcelo Caetano, they installed General António Spinola as the new head of state. Spinola wished to end the African wars but had no intention of granting independence to the colonies. Instead, he envisioned a Lusophonic commonwealth in which Mozambique, Angola, Guinea-Bissau, and Cabo

Verde would remain under Lisbon's control with some measure of local autonomy.

Samora and his comrades were caught off guard. Even as word of the coup arrived, they were mapping out the next phase in the guerrilla war, which they assumed would last another decade. As Oscar Monteiro remembered,

> We were in Nachingwea and it was around nine thirty in the morning. We were taking a break between the classes. Gideon Ndobe rushed in to announce that he just heard on shortwave radio that there might have been a military takeover in Lisbon. . . . By one p.m., Samora had gathered the FRELIMO Executive Committee and officers from the general staff to formulate our response. Within a few hours we had prepared a statement in which we affirmed our support for the democratic forces in Portugal, but we insisted that we did not take up arms to become black Portuguese in a liberal democracy. Until Lisbon agreed to Mozambican independence, we would continue the armed struggle.[50]

Two months later, the Armed Forces Movement proposed an immediate cease-fire. At a meeting in Lusaka organized by President Kaunda of Zambia, Mario Soares, Portugal's new socialist foreign minister, reiterated his call for an end to the fighting and a national referendum to determine Mozambique's future. Although Kaunda endorsed this proposal, FRELIMO rejected it because it failed to recognize either that the Mozambican people had the right to be independent or that power should immediately be transferred to

FRELIMO. Unable to resolve their differences, the parties agreed to meet again in the coming months.

In the interim, Samora instituted a three-pronged military, diplomatic, and psychological campaign. He ordered the general command to intensify the war effort by opening a new front in Zambézia, the colony's most populous province. Approximately a thousand Portuguese troops deserted there in the face of FRELIMO attacks. In August, FRELIMO scored a major victory in Cabo Delgado. Employing the most sophisticated weapons in its arsenal, including Russian artillery and rocket launchers, guerrillas bombarded the Portuguese stronghold at Milele, capturing 126 colonial troops. While Portuguese negotiators insisted that storming the base was a violation of the spirit of Lusaka, Samora maintained that the cease-fire was predicated on Lisbon's willingness to accept a transfer of power.[51] The Portuguese chief of staff, for his part, admitted the armed forces no longer had the will to fight.[52]

At the same time, Samora traveled to the Organization of African Unity's meeting in Mogadishu to garner support. His position was that, given the shift in power, the time for a referendum had long passed: "One does not ask a slave if he wants to be free, especially after he has rebelled, and still less if one is a slave owner."[53]

Samora also reached out to Mozambique's Portuguese community with a plea for reconciliation without recrimination. In a radio broadcast beamed into Mozambique from Tanzania, Samora affirmed that "FRELIMO belongs to the Mozambican people," and that "in our ranks, there is room and work for every Mozambican woman and man, for all those who wish to be Mozambicans, including those who, although not born here, want to experience and build the new Mozambique."[54]

After a secret meeting in Holland initiated by the Portuguese, negotiations reconvened in Lusaka.[55] FRELIMO demanded independence and rejected any role for anti-FRELIMO African organizations, maintaining that they lacked popular support and their presence would ultimately lead to a neocolonial arrangement.[56] In the end, Portuguese negotiators acquiesced, but FRELIMO had to accept important economic concessions, including Lisbon's right to retain ownership and control over the giant dam at Cahora Bassa until Mozambique repaid the $500 million debt Portugal had incurred by building it.[57] Thus, FRELIMO was unable to break the colonial chains of dependency—leading Aquino de Bragança, one of Samora's advisers, to warn that Mozambique could end up like many other African nations, with "independence but not decolonization."[58]

Reconvening in Lusaka on September 7, 1974, the Armed Forces Movement agreed to a transfer of power to FRELIMO within the year. Thirteen days later a transitional government, led by Joaquim Chissano and composed of six representatives of FRELIMO and four Portuguese officials, was installed in Lourenço Marques.

Despite Samora's guarantees, news of the Lusaka Accord unleashed immediate fears in Mozambique's Portuguese community. On the day of the signing, right-wing settlers calling themselves Fico (I am staying) and Dragões da Morte (Dragons of Death) launched an abortive coup in the capital. Supported by some Portuguese commandos and PIDE officials, they captured the radio station and newspaper and blew up an arsenal on the outskirts of the city. Shantytown residents rose up against this putsch and an estimated sixty civilians were killed and more than 450 wounded before a joint force of Portuguese and FRELIMO troops crushed the rebellion three days later.

On the eve of independence, with rumors circulating of an impending South African or Rhodesian invasion, Samora went on the radio and warned that such aggression would evoke a response by FRELIMO's allies. While no attack materialized, the Ian Smith regime in Rhodesia began recruiting Africans who had worked for PIDE or served in its elite commando force, Flechas (Arrows). This was the origin of the Mozambican National Resistance, predecessor of RENAMO, which would create havoc in the new nation during the next decade.

FRELIMO continued to face internal opposition. Separatist movements such as the União Nacional Africana de Rombézia sought to detach northern Mozambique from the rest of the country, and the Fico white settler movement remained active. These groups received support from Malawi, Rhodesia, and elements in the Portuguese military. It was even rumored the CIA was trying to resurrect the Comite Revolucionário de Moçambique, an allegation the American embassy denied.[59] The militantly anticommunist archbishop of Lourenço Marques, Custódio Alvim Pereira, urged from his pulpit that Africans must "love your land which is Mozambique integrated with Portugal" and warned that "the present African liberation movements are against the church."[60] Nationalists such as Uria Simango also continued to insist that political and economic power be in the hands of the African majority, and that FRELIMO represented the interests of whites, mulattoes, and *assimilados*.

Samora acknowledged that these explosive issues were not just a remnant of the past. On the eve of independence he wrote, "In the course of the struggle our great victory has been in transforming the armed struggle for national liberation into a revolution. In other words, our final aim in the struggle is not to hoist a flag different from the Portuguese, or ... to put a Black president into the Ponto Vermelha Palace in Lourenço Marques instead of a White governor. We say our aim is to win complete independence, establish people's power, build a new society without exploitation, for the benefit of all those who identify as Mozambicans."[61]

He then embarked on a month-long journey in an old prop airplane from the Rovuma River in the far north to the Maputo River in the south. Traveling with his son Samito and Nyeleti Mondlane, the daughter of his assassinated predecessor, he landed in every province, visiting cities and towns to win over skeptics. Samora knew how to read his audience. At the site of the Mueda massacre he spoke reassuringly, addressing the apparent diffidence of his audience: "It seems as if everybody's afraid, but the administrators aren't here anymore, right? Yesterday it was the bomb that made a noise, but now it is our victory."[62]

For most Mozambicans, the unimaginable was happening. A black man was taking the reins of power. Not any black man, but one dressed in guerrilla garb who understood their suffering and their dreams for the future, who not only spoke from the podium but enthusiastically waded into crowds to embrace the elders and dance with all, young and old.

His speech on June 14th in the strategic city of Beira, a colonial stronghold and home to a loose coalition of anti-FRELIMO forces and white settler groups, revealed Samora's oratorical skills. Thousands, many from surrounding shantytowns, came to hear him. He addressed the audience in what Colin Darch and David Hedges have called "Mozambican Portuguese—a liberating language spoken in short and repetitive phrases, simplified grammar fused with words, images and rhythm from African languages."[63] At various points he connected with the audience by asking, after each statement, if he was accurately describing the oppression they had experienced under colonialism.

On the evening of June 24, 1975, thousands of Mozambicans poured into Machava Stadium in the capital to watch the lowering of the Portuguese flag and the transfer of power to FRELIMO. Samora led the crowd in the national anthem while Alberto Chipande, who had fired the first shot at Chai, raised the Mozambican flag. With family members, friends, and militants cheering wildly, Samora declared "the total and complete independence of Mozambique." Pandemonium broke out, people wept, and celebrations erupted throughout the country among those who had been listening by radio. Raul Honwana, father of four FRELIMO militants, summed up the collective euphoria within the stadium: "At zero hour on the 25th of June, at seventy years of age, I witnessed with incredible emotions the moment of the independence proclamation of the sovereign nation of Mozambique."[64]

This must have been a bittersweet moment for Samora. His dream of a free Mozambique had been realized. He had become the embodiment of the revolution: in South Africa, black students who considered him their champion as well yelled out his name while rejoicing in the streets of Durban and at the University of the North.[65]

Samora, however, had paid a heavy personal price. He had suffered the loss of many comrades, including Mondlane and Josina. He had not seen his four older children for many years. Two months earlier, his mother had passed away,[66] and his dream of sharing this moment with her died as well. Above all else, Samora was acutely aware of the pressing problems his government would need to address the following day.

Politics, Performance, and People's Power, 1975–ca. 1977

On the eve of independence, the FRELIMO Central Committee had ratified Mozambique's first constitution, which affirmed that its president would be the president of the nation. To distinguish the liberation movement from the political party into which it morphed, it became common practice to refer to the party as "Frelimo."

At forty-two, President Samora was entering uncharted waters as he and his newly appointed government faced both inherited problems and new challenges. The next morning, as the first order of business, Samora and senior military officials met with a Chinese delegation over breakfast, during which he tried unsuccessfully to obtain sophisticated weapons to protect the new nation from attacks by Rhodesia and South Africa.

Like other newly independent countries in Africa, Mozambique faced illiteracy, poverty, ethnic and regional cleavages, underdevelopment, and the challenge of organizing a state capable of remedying these ills. Other problems, including a number with which FRELIMO had already grappled, arose specifically from the Mozambican experience. How would Frelimo create a sense of national unity and overcome a history of ethnic and regional particularism that had been heightened by colonial propaganda? How should it deal with emotionally charged issues of race and national identity? How could it translate the popular support it already enjoyed in liberated regions and among clandestine supporters, particularly in Lourenço Marques, to other parts of the country, when there was no longer a common oppressor?

Samora's promise to avoid the pitfalls of "tribalism" and neocolonialism also posed serious ideological and practical questions. How would a front whose members were sometimes at odds over their vision of an independent Mozambique build a nation out of disparate populations, many of which had limited contact with each other? How would Frelimo give meaning to the somewhat vague notion of People's Power? What were the most effective ways of transforming Mozambique's colonial economy, established to serve the metropole, into one that served the Mozambican people—especially given the flight of Portuguese settlers who had enjoyed a near monopoly on education and filled all the managerial positions?

Ongoing threats from Rhodesia and South Africa made finding solutions for these issues appreciably more difficult. Both white regimes saw independent black African states on their borders as existential threats. During the armed struggle, Rhodesia had sent troops into Mozambique to fight alongside the Portuguese and had created the Mozambique National Resistance—composed primarily of disgruntled FRELIMO members, former colonial soldiers, and other collaborators with the Portuguese—which engaged in terrorist acts even before the ink on the Lusaka Accord was dry. Shortly after independence, Magnus Malan, chief of the South African Defense Force, warned President Machel that, "if threatened," his troops could occupy the capital in less than a day. The apartheid regime's fears about Frelimo were well founded. During the 1976 Soweto uprising, high school students took to the streets chanting the Frelimo slogan, *A luta continua*, a graphic reminder that Mozambique's liberation had captured the imagination of South Africa's young militants.

Now, in speeches, writings, and interviews, Samora focused on the challenges of nation- and state-building and transforming Mozambican society. Both the power of his ideas and the style of his public performance captivated his followers and advanced Frelimo's program. This far-reaching agenda, however, was not Samora's alone. While he was the face of the nation and first among equals, the Frelimo leadership included other critical thinkers and strong personalities—Marcelino dos Santos, Joaquim Chissano, Armando Guebuza, Jorge Rebelo, and Oscar Monteiro, to name a few—who had their own ideas about the revolution's path. All were members of the Frelimo Political Bureau, which gave direction to the party, shaped state policy, and directed ministries.

Samora vigorously promoted social reforms in education, health, and housing, and was a proponent of gender equality. He looked to support from socialist allies to enable the newly independent nation to overcome the crushing realities of an overwhelmingly poor and underdeveloped country surrounded by hostile neighbors. Additionally, he sought to construct a modern society in which the voices, interests, and aspirations of peasants and workers would shape his new government's policies. These principles embodied Samora's notion of People's Power.

Instituting People's Power was a tall order, however, and Samora was an impatient leader. He was unwilling to tamp down his expectations or tolerate corruption. He fought to achieve these objectives, but in his haste to transform society Samora often underestimated social complexities on the ground. The lessons of the liberated zone, the socialist vision expressed through speeches and posters, his personal popularity, and the euphoria of the moment were insufficient to ensure radical transformation. Thus, his administration rarely fulfilled his most ambitious goals.

Nevertheless, during the first years after independence, life for most Mozambicans improved. Gone were the colonial political structures that had instilled fear in their daily lives—although state abuses of power persisted on a smaller scale in the name of enforcing Frelimo's revolutionary and moralistic dictates. In independent Mozambique, Africans were no longer beaten in the fields, humiliated at work, or denied entrance to restaurants, sports clubs, or theaters. They rarely suffered racial indignities and were not forced to live in segregated shantytowns or strategic hamlets enclosed in barbed wire. Millions of Mozambicans now had access to the education and health care previously available to only an elite few. For Mozambicans of Asian descent, there was no fear of expulsion, as was occurring in Uganda and Kenya.

The political, social, and economic transformations Samora's government initiated were organically connected, and policies pursued in one domain had profound and sometimes unintended or contradictory effects on other aspects of Mozambican life. While people were encouraged to vote in local elections, Frelimo outlawed all rival parties. Campaigns to abolish polygamy and bride-wealth, which had an emancipatory impact on millions of women, alienated many men, traditionalists, and some older women. Meanwhile, the commitment to neighboring liberation struggles—supported by most Mozambicans—triggered a reign of terror through much of the countryside, backed by Rhodesia and South Africa, that devastated many Frelimo initiatives.

Samora also faced the personal challenge of reconstituting his family, most of whom he had not seen for more than a decade. His five children lived in three different households, and most were only informed of their father's identity on the eve of independence, making this more difficult. Olívia Machel, his third-oldest child, first heard about Samora when he was being vilified by the Portuguese in state-controlled media as a "notorious terrorist leader." As she later recalled, "I was born in 1961 and my father left when I was less than two. I had no memory of him. We had no communication. My maternal uncle changed my last name and that of my sibling to Tchikomo to protect us from PIDE. In 1973, our mother explained that Samora and FRELIMO were not terrorists but fighting for Mozambican independence. A year later, my paternal grandmother came to Lourenço Marques for health treatment and told me that Samora was my father."[1]

Building a Nation

Like many other African countries, Mozambique's boundaries had been arbitrarily delineated during colonial-era negotiations between Portugal, Britain, and Germany. Their agreements completely disregarded the histories and cultures of the multiple ethnic groups residing in Mozambique, whose members maintained their social identities into the postindependence period.

The challenge of nation-building was further complicated by Frelimo's weak presence in much of the central and southern half of the country—especially in Beira and Maputo, Mozambique's two major cities, where colonial values and practices were most deeply entrenched and a variety of opposition groups were still trying to subvert its legitimacy. Millions of Mozambicans had only the vaguest idea of Frelimo's message and ideology, requiring Samora's government to rapidly create a new social cohesion that would bind individuals of diverse communities, religions, and ethnic groups to the emerging nation. Samora recognized that this new "imagined community" was both a political and cultural artifact—difficult to construct and even harder to sustain.[2]

In his speech on Independence Day, transmitted by radio across the country, Samora had passionately addressed the meaning of national identity and citizenship. "We do not recognize tribes, region, race or religious beliefs. We only recognize Mozambicans who are equally exploited and equally desirous of freedom and revolution." Underscoring the dangers that these prior loyalties posed to the new nation, he warned, "to be united, it is not enough to state that one is united. It is necessary to wage a constant battle against all divisive situations and tendencies."[3]

The principle that citizenship was not contingent on origin or skin color was enshrined in Mozambique's new constitution, which outlawed all acts creating divisions or privileged positions based on race, gender, ethnic origin, or class position. Immediately after independence Frelimo initiated campaigns against ethnic regionalism, racism, and sexism. Broadcasts, newspaper articles, comic strips, bulletin boards, murals, and graffiti stressed the message that "from the Rovuma to the Maputo, we are all Mozambicans."

Deeds, more than slogans, however, demonstrated this commitment. One example illustrates Samora's commitment to spreading the benefits of independence. Shortly after independence, Fidel Castro offered to train nine hundred Mozambicans as doctors, engineers, and scientists. After convincing Castro to raise that number to twelve thousand over the course of a decade, Samora announced that 120 young men and women of all races and religions would be selected annually in each of Mozambique's ten provinces to train in Cuba and then return to their provinces to work.[4] This was a first step in closing the educational gap between northern and southern Mozambicans, the latter of whom had historically had more access to education. He also arranged for other students to advance their education in Eastern Europe.

Nonracialism was another central component of Frelimo's vision. When we arrived in Maputo in 1977, one of the first things we noticed was an enormous poster depicting black and white arms embracing. Its caption read "Abaixo com racismo" ("Down with racism").

Samora selected prominent guerrillas and clandestine supporters of FRELIMO regardless of race to fill senior positions in his administration, including the cabinet and senior provincial appointees. The twenty-person cabinet included fifteen Africans and *mestiços*, three white Mozambicans, and two of Goan descent. The faces of the ministers figured prominently in the national media, reinforcing the message that Mozambique was becoming a nonracial society.

In stark contrast, women were conspicuously absent from state and party leadership. Rhetoric about gender equality and the need to include women in all aspects of the revolutionary struggle did not translate into access to the inner circles of power. There was only one woman in the first cabinet—Samora's fiancé, Graça Simbine, who was named minister of education.[5]

Building a nation was a cultural as well as a political process. Societal transformation required popularizing the cultural dimensions of the nation's diverse ethnic groups, making them part of the national consciousness, while internalizing revolutionary values. Samora promoted the view that this synthesis was the key to creating a distinct Mozambican identity. As he put it in one speech, "Let art seek to combine old forms with new content, then giving rise to new forms. Let painting, written literature, theater and the artistic handicraft be added to the traditional culture, dance, sculpture and singing. Let the creativity of some become that of all, men, women, young and old, from the north to the south, so that the all new revolutionary Mozambican culture may be born to all."[6]

Such public exhortations were an essential feature of Samora's effort to "perform the nation"—a task he relished.[7] A charismatic leader and natural orator, he was at his best in large outdoor meetings. On stage, dressed in guerrilla fatigues, with his swagger, infectious smile, and biting sarcasm on full display, he left his audiences entranced. Samora understood the power of imagery and the appeal to national pride his performances evoked. According to Luís Bernardo Honwana, Samora's chief of staff, he relished the fact that he was the embodiment of the revolution, inspiring hope for the future of the nation.[8] His characteristic use of singing to engage his listeners led Fidel Castro to exclaim that Samora was "the first leader I've seen who can bring order to the masses through revolutionary songs."[9]

A careful reading of Samora's speeches and writings reveals an emancipatory project laced with puritanical undertones reflecting his missionary education. In speech after speech, he stressed moral rectitude, appropriate comportment, and self-discipline. One historian has said Samora's speeches "read like evangelical sermons . . . a moral crusade as well as a political revolution."[10]

Simply reading Samora's speeches fails to capture the complexity of his performances. His repertoire included the intentional use of repetition, incorrect grammar, body language, and engagement with the audience through song, humor, and sarcasm. He intuitively understood that songs evoke powerful emotions and memories, instill a sense of purpose, self-confidence, and power in the listeners, and create a deep personal bond with them.

On several occasions, we attended rallies in which Samora silenced the crowd's murmuring by breaking into "Kanimambo, FRELIMO" (Thank you, FRELIMO), singing each stanza in a different African language. This would be followed by one or two other songs, most commonly "Não vamos esquecer" (We will never forget) or "O povo organizado" (The people organized), with crowds singing along or humming the melody. Then Samora would raise his voice and shout a revolutionary slogan: "*Abaixo com Apartheid*" (Down with apartheid) or "*Abaixo com Xiconhoca*" (Down with Xiconhoca—a cartoon character embodying all that was corrupt or immoral about colonialism that continued to exist in the new Mozambique). The crowd shouted back, "*Abaixo!*" So convincing were his performances that Kok Nam, Mozambique's leading photographer who regularly accompanied Samora, was heard to brag that "Samora could even convince a cadaver."[11]

As the Mozambican journalist Carlos Cardoso recalled, "When the people talk of our president, they don't say 'Samora Moisés Machel, president of Frelimo, president of the People's Republic of Mozambique.' The people say 'Samora,' or 'Comrade President'... with joy, because they feel, they know, that he is their comrade."[12] Perhaps Beira resident Pinto de Abreu summed up best how Samora touched the lives of ordinary Mozambicans. Forty years after meeting Samora while on his way to study in Cuba, he still remembered and cherished their brief encounter: "This day was great for me, not only because I had come so close to Samora ... but especially because I was touched by his loving greeting. Samora naturally affects with his character, with his magnetic presence. It was not a gesture of political fabrication or charm that had been rehearsed the day before, it was something that came spontaneously from within him, from the heart."[13]

Samora periodically stepped out of his role as father of the nation and moral guardian to work alongside ordinary Mozambicans. In 1977, he was featured on the cover of *Tempo*, the country's leading weekly magazine, harvesting rice at a state farm in Gaza along with thousands of volunteers from Maputo. Newspapers and billboards regularly showed him laboring side-by-side with peasants and workers.[14] Such images projected to the nation Samora's belief that work and human dignity were inextricably intertwined. Photographs like these were important building blocks in Frelimo's nationalist and socialist iconography.[15]

Building a State: Postcolonial Politics

To build a nation required a strong and effective state serving the common good. The skills needed to engage in guerrilla struggle and those required to construct a state were very different. In a moment of self-reflection during his Beira speech immediately before independence, Samora acknowledged the enormity of this task, while maintaining his confidence in the ultimate success of the revolution: "The truth is that we fully understand what we do not want—oppression, exploitation, humiliation—but, as to what we want and how to get it, our ideas are necessarily still vague. They are born out of practice, corrected by practice. We undoubtedly will run into setbacks. But it is from these setbacks that we will learn."[16]

Frelimo had little governing experience and only a minimal presence in many parts of the country. Samora was acutely aware of the country's small number of economists, medical personnel, jurists, and diplomats. He recognized that many of the most qualified cadres were in their late twenties and thirties, with little practical knowledge of how to organize the ministries to which they were appointed or to govern in the provinces.[17] For all of these reasons, he admonished against romanticizing the armed struggle and exhorted militants not to succumb to triumphalism. Complacency, he warned, would undermine the revolution.[18]

To mobilize Mozambicans in their rural communities, urban neighborhoods, and workplaces was a task beyond the capacity of the relatively small number of Frelimo cadres. The critical job of mobilizing the masses fell to grassroots organizations known as *grupos dinamizadores* (dynamizing groups), which were first implemented in Nachingwea during the war. Dynamizing groups generally consisted of approximately a dozen elected Frelimo sympathizers. For Samora, this was the essence of People's Power.

We attended several meetings in our Maputo neighborhood organized by our local dynamizing group. To us, the meetings seemed freewheeling, unruly, and time-consuming. Nevertheless, they did provide an opportunity for frank, sometimes heated, discussions on a wide array of issues affecting the community. Participants raised concerns ranging from family disputes and conflicts with their neighbors to larger social problems such as poor sanitary conditions, price gouging, crime, and prostitution. Dynamizing groups also organized neighborhood work parties and cultural events and encouraged community members to attend plays, marches, and rallies celebrating the new Mozambique.

Two of their most important functions were transmitting Frelimo ideology and serving as Frelimo's eyes and ears. They explained and led discussions of state policies, promoted patriotism, and denounced suspected enemies of the revolution. Roberta Washington, an American architect working in the Ministry of Housing, described what transpired during dynamizing group meetings there, held every Saturday from 8:00 a.m. to noon: "Cooperantes [like Washington] did not need to attend, but I was curious about what took place, so I regularly attended. Sometimes, it was Marxist theory made boring by people not that good at explaining it. But mostly, it was a time to talk and get to hang out with colleagues and friends. Except during that period when Mozambicans who were suspected to have worked with PIDE were being made to 'confess' before everyone; then, it was just downright eerie."[19] Despite the tendency of men to dominate these meetings, the inefficiencies, and the occasional misuses of power, the dynamizing groups were widely accepted.

Before Frelimo could construct a strong and effective state, it had to dismantle colonial institutions. One of the first targets was the colonial police force. To replace it, Samora's administration encouraged the creation of militias in neighborhoods and workplaces. The mandate of these People's Vigilance Groups was "to neutralize enemy action, defend vital points of the economic productive sector, and detect infiltrators aiming to undermine the economy and state apparatus." Many joined for patriotic reasons—to defend against traitors and guard strategic sites—while others volunteered to protect their communities from criminals, alcoholics, and drug abusers. Members also derived very real benefits, including preferred access to ration cards.[20] The militia members' poor training, relative autonomy, and revolutionary fervor sometimes led to abuses of power. Overzealous members arrested citizens for minor infractions like noise-making and public displays of affection. Women wearing miniskirts and high heels were presumed to be sex workers and were frequent targets.[21]

Another colonial institution that was an early target was the judicial system. Under postindependence legal reforms, Africans for the first time had their cases tried in a court of their peers. This was a radical departure from their past experiences, in which capricious colonial authorities and state-appointed chiefs applied some combination of "customary law" and the colonial penal code.

Samora's government also rejected widescale use of incarceration to punish those who violated societal norms, Instead, reeducation centers were established shortly after independence. Samora's faith in revolutionary pedagogy and restorative justice shaped his thinking about the reeducation process, which dated back to the armed struggle.[22] Moral and political education and the development of a work ethic would serve as the basis for rehabilitation. Samora articulated this vision in the following terms: "The reeducation center should be a school where professional knowledge should be passed on and made use of. It is the fundamental task of officials in charge of reeducation centers to know the history of each one of the people being re-educated—his life history and his origin—in order to understand why he committed his crimes."[23]

Although reeducation camps dated back to the armed struggle, the actual organization and functioning of these centers in the postindependence period bore little relationship to Samora's vision. He appointed Armando Guebuza, Frelimo's political commissar and a very harsh disciplinarian, to oversee them. Under his direction, more than fifteen thousand Mozambican citizens were detained in the first years of independence for minor offenses or inappropriate behavior, including beer brewing, prostitution, and petty crimes. Many were arbitrarily incarcerated. To this group were added old and new Frelimo dissidents and opponents of the regime. Thus, even as the legal system was being restructured to allow Africans to have their day in court, many "enemies of the revolution" were being severely punished without trial.

Although the state outlawed political parties other than Frelimo, voting was an important component of People's Power because it engaged citizens in the political process. All Mozambicans except those who had worked for the secret police or other repressive colonial institutions had the right to vote. Between September and December 1977, more than twenty-two thousand men and women—all professed supporters of Frelimo—were elected to serve as deputies in 894 local elections.[24] A *New York Times* reporter observing the election process noted, "If enthusiasm has waned in other places [in Africa], it is palpable here. . . . There is evidence that the degree of mobilization and national purpose attained here is great and may be more durable than anything black Africa has known."[25]

Nevertheless, the levers of power were pressed behind closed doors. Critical meetings of the National Council of Ministers and the Central Committee of the Political Bureau were closed to the public and press, making it impossible to determine the scope and intensity of debate and the extent of ideological faultlines, competing factions and court intrigues. Thus, until the last years of Samora's rule Frelimo presented a united front. Meanwhile, within this tightly knit circle, Samora could instill fear as well as admiration. One confidante noted that, on occasion, we "were all fearful of a quiet, non-talkative Samora with his cutting gaze."[26]

The memoir of Helder Martins, Mozambique's first minister of health, provides a glimpse of Samora's dominant role in his brief description of the Council of Ministers' debate about nationalizing the health system. Martins had been instructed by Samora to develop a long-term strategy. After studying the problem for over a year, he proposed delaying implementation because of logistical challenges and shortages of trained personnel. Samora asked each member of the council to comment, listening carefully and asking many questions. After they had all agreed with Martins, Samora opined that, if the government did not act immediately, "in two years' time everyone would have arguments to seek a new postponement." In the end, Samora prevailed.[27]

Samora was clearly first among equals. Nevertheless, there are several documented instances of ministers speaking out against his favored positions. In 1978, Joaquim Carvalho, minister of agriculture, opposed

Samora's plan to support the private family sector as well as large state farms.[28] On another occasion, Teodato Hunguana, minister of justice, wrote a confidential memo to Samora disagreeing with his decision to reinstate corporal punishment, including the colonial practice of whipping.[29] Both ministers were sacked, although they were later appointed to different senior positions.

At times, however, Samora was a good listener. He often invited individuals or small groups to the presidential palace where, over after-dinner drinks, he encouraged them to air their concerns or sought their advice. On several occasions he even reconsidered policies already in place, when convinced they were misguided or ineffective. Several years after Carvalho's dismissal, João Ferreira, then the minister of agriculture, lobbied successfully for scarce resources to be redistributed from the failing communal village system to family agriculture.[30] Aquino de Bragança, a free-thinking Frelimo intellectual, was notorious for disagreeing with the president on a range of issues in closed-door meetings. And despite Samora's tendency to view the press with suspicion, the maverick reporter Carlos Cardoso could pose challenging questions in public, confident that he would not be denied future access. According to Graça Machel, Samora appreciated Cardoso's intellect and willingness to spar with the president.[31]

One of the hallmarks of political life under Samora was the absence of corruption or accumulation of personal wealth by the country's leaders. Samora dressed well, but he had neither Swiss bank accounts nor palaces, yachts, or overseas properties. High-level government and party officials maintained an equally unpretentious lifestyle, although they did live appreciably better than the average Mozambican citizen. They resided in state-owned homes abandoned by wealthy Portuguese and had access to special state stores where they could purchase commodities not generally available.[32] The "children of the revolution" also had access to the best education and health facilities in Mozambique and abroad.

In the same vein, members of official delegations traveling abroad received only three dollars per day for discretionary expenses, while the head of the mission received two dollars more. In the words of one former minister, the "amount was hardly enough to purchase trinkets for my children."[33] Before visiting Swaziland, we once asked a friend who happened to be the wife of a senior minister if she wanted us to buy anything for her. She replied sheepishly that she would love some biltong (beef jerky) but had no hard currency to pay for it. José Luís Cabaço remembered that during his tenure as minister of information he was forced to ask an Italian acquaintance to purchase microphone batteries that his ministry badly needed, because he lacked the foreign currency to do so himself.[34]

Transforming Society

As a young man, Samora was heavily influenced by Frantz Fanon's contention that "colonizing the mind" was the most insidious legacy of colonialism. In his 1977 acceptance speech upon receiving an honorary doctor of law degree from Nigeria's Ahmadu Bello University, Samora emphasized that "the ultimate effort [of colonialism was] to make out of each Mozambican an

Figure 5.1. Samora speaking at independence celebration.
Courtesy of Centro de Documentção e Formação Fotográfica
(CDFF)

Figure 5.2. Samora and father. Courtesy of Centro
de Documentação Samora Machel (CDSM)

Figure 5.3. Samora speaking at a rally. (CDFF)

Figure 5.4. Samora with students. Courtesy of António Alves Gomes

Figure 5.5. Samora with Presidents Julius Nyerere, Kenneth Kaunda, and Seretse Khama. Courtesy of António Alves Gomes

Figure 5.6. Wedding of Samora and Graça Machel. (CDSM)

Figure 5.7. Samora dancing up a storm. (CDSM)

Figure 5.8. Samora meeting with Portuguese president António Eanes. (CDFF)

assimilado, a little Portuguese with a black skin" and defined colonialism as a cultural act of rape.[35] He believed the democratization of knowledge would free Mozambicans from the shackles of illiteracy, the tyranny of superstition, and the cultural arrogance of missionary education. Learning was a social act reinforced through daily practice in the household, community, and workplace, and the family was the most significant institution of instruction: "All of us have responsibilities. We educate our children, we educate our youth in various ways. The behavior of parents, the way they live at home is more significant than the five hours [a day] that students are in contact with their teachers."[36]

Samora's ideological position and pragmatism made him a strong proponent of liberating girls and women through education. In public meetings across the country, he joined representatives of the Mozambican Women's Organization to chastise parents who kept their daughters at home to work on the family's fields and prepare for marriage, thus keeping them ignorant and dependent and depriving the nation of a well-trained labor force.

Under the direction of Graça Machel, Samora's administration embarked on a program to expand access to education and reorganize the curriculum. In an interview with Allen and Iain Christie, Samora proudly cited statistics demonstrating that "today education is for everyone . . . [and] free. In 1973 there were 588,868 attending schools. Five years later it had increased by more than 100 percent."[37] The new curriculum eliminated discussion of the heroic exploits of Henry the Navigator and the civilizing mission of the Catholic Church.

Instead, it emphasized Mozambique's rich heritage, its long tradition of resistance, and the church's collaboration with the colonial state to obliterate its past.[38]

The unholy alliance of the Catholic Church and the colonial state, which had deleteriously shaped Samora's own development, convinced him to nationalize church property in 1976 and eliminate its stranglehold on African education. The policy pained many Christian supporters of Frelimo and alienated others.[39]

Samora also stressed the strategic importance of adult literacy. That more than 90 percent of Mozambicans could neither read nor write, he argued, deprived both them and the nation of the results of their creative potential. Colonial values and "irrational and unscientific ideas from the past" froze Mozambicans in a permanent state of backwardness.[40]

Universal education and widespread literacy campaigns were critical elements of Frelimo's cultural politics, embodied in the twin notions of *Moçambicanidade* (Mozambican-ness) and *o Homen Novo* (the New Man)—ideas the liberation movement first developed in Nachingwea.

Moçambicanidade was a synthesis of indigenous cultural practices with a new revolutionary content.[41] In 1977, high school students and researchers from Eduardo Mondlane University traveled the countryside collecting local traditions, histories, songs, and dances and identifying important archeological sites. The government organized cultural festivals that brought together representatives from all parts of the country. Although forging a unified culture remained largely aspirational, these initiatives did have an impact on the ground, particularly in Maputo. The director of the National Song and Dance Company (CNCD) wrote about the significance of culture in the nation-building process.

> The encouragement of dance in a country engulfed by war and famine might seem like sacrilege. Yet in Mozambique, dance is life. The nation has long discovered and expressed itself in terms of dance—dance by villagers for the victorious guerrilla fighters in the long war for independence against Portuguese colonialism, dance by triumphant soldiers themselves to celebrate independence in 1975, and then a vast postindependence dance festival ("the people in motion").... Today every factory, school, hospital, and farming enterprise has its dance groups. In the community, the people drum and dance—dance is communication, dance is affirmation, dance is criticism, and dance is simply dance.[42]

Believing that from this cultural synthesis would emerge the New Man—guardian of the revolution and guarantor against future backsliding—Samora stressed that "even when the systems of exploitation have been destroyed, if we do not fight the mentality underlying them, then sooner or later, slowly or rapidly, the system will spring up again, nourished by the negative values preserved within us." The New Man would be militant, hardworking, proud of his identity, history, and culture, educated in modern science, and reject the obscurantist and exploitative practices of the past. He would be respectful to women and opposed to bride-price and polygamy.[43] Still, this formulation nowhere addressed the enduring privilege of patriarchy.

The New Man was the antithesis of the cartoon character Xiconhoca. The name was a combination of "Chico," a notorious PIDE official, and *nhoca* (snake), and the character represented the enemy within, preying upon unknowing, defenseless individuals. In comics, posters, and bulletin boards set up in every administrative center, Xiconhoca was variously portrayed as an insensitive bureaucrat complicating the lives of the people, a citizen who refused to work, a pimp, drug dealer, or prostitute, a woman who wore miniskirts and high-heeled shoes, a young person who partied at nightclubs, a polygamist, a parent who failed to send children to school, or a traitor spying for South Africa or Rhodesia.

There were also radical changes to the health-care system. Less than a month after independence Samora announced the nationalization of medicine, making medical care a right of citizenship rather than a commercial venture fraught with racism. Implementing such a far-reaching program with only eighty-seven doctors in the country was a major challenge. By 1977, the Ministry of Health had recruited more than five hundred foreign medical workers from over twenty nations. In subsequent years, drawing on the examples of China and Vietnam, the government continued to bring hundreds of "barefoot doctors" and infirmaries to the countryside. This enabled it to launch a vaccination campaign against measles, smallpox, and tetanus that reached 90 percent of the country during the next two years. The World Health Organization declared it one of the most successful initiatives in Africa.[44] Another preventative initiative was the latrine campaign to reduce cholera and other waterborne diseases. Samora proclaimed two successive Sundays in 1977 as National Latrine Days and, with pickaxe and spade, joined other citizens digging and building latrines. Thanks to these and other measures, the estimated 20 percent decline in infant mortality during the first five years of independence suggests the degree to which Mozambique's new health system was making inroads.[45]

Frelimo also nationalized rental properties to prevent urban landlords from profiting from apartment blocks left vacant by Portuguese who had fled Mozambique. The new legislation also targeted black slumlords in the shantytowns. In Maputo alone, more than fifty thousand units were nationalized.[46] Within the next two years, more than 160,000 Mozambicans living in substandard housing had been relocated to urban residences taken over by the state.[47]

Although initial accomplishments in the social sphere were substantial, these ambitious policies were never fully implemented. Even with the budget sharply increased, dramatic rises in the number of students meant there were never enough schools, trained teachers, books, and supplies.[48] The nationalized health-care delivery system similarly strained the state's capacity. Newly built rural infirmaries were inadequately staffed and supplied and the widely hailed "barefoot doctors" were often not up to the task. Nationalizing housing without sufficient oversight enabled corrupt bureaucrats to allocate the best housing to their friends, families, and those willing to offer bribes. The loss of their rental income had the unintended consequence of increasing the flight of skilled Portuguese who, Samora had hoped, would continue to keep the economy going.

The cultural politics Samora promoted were also problematic. Cultures are not divisible, and traditions are not frozen artifacts of the past. Samora's efforts to preserve many aspects of the past while abolishing traditional chiefs and attacking polygamy ignored the complexities of local culture and generated antipathy toward the new government, especially in the countryside. His attack on the church also alienated many devout Christians who were also fervent nationalists.

Economic Transformations

Few newly independent nations inherited as many deeply embedded economic problems as Mozambique, with its already low level of food production, high unemployment rate, embryonic industrial sector, negative balance of payments, and extremely low gross national product.[49] These factors were all negatively affected by the mass exodus of Portuguese, whose number dropped from 250,000 to 20,000 between 1974 and 1976. Gone were the vast majority of the country's engineers, accountants, mechanics, and agronomists. Departing settlers frequently destroyed what they could not take with them, sabotaging everything from trucks to factory equipment, from tractors to trains.

Between 1975 and 1977 the government took numerous steps to reverse the economic hemorrhaging. By nationalizing abandoned farms and plantations and reorganizing them into large state farms, jobs were preserved for thousands of rural workers. To prevent their total collapse, the government nationalized strategic industries and took control of mismanaged firms. It established *lojas do povo* (people's shops) to ensure that poor people had access to basic commodities at subsidized prices. These interventions were more tactical than ideological—a response to economic breakdown and fear of paralysis.[50]

Under pressure from the Mozambican Women's Organization and feminist critics, Samora introduced policies to combat the institutional oppression of women and create new opportunities in the workplace. Urban women made small but significant breakthroughs, for the first time finding employment as tractor drivers, construction workers, police officers, and administrators. Women also constituted nearly half of the students selected to study in Cuba to be trained as engineers, doctors, dentists, teachers, and other professionals.[51]

Nonetheless, women who entered the workforce still encountered gender discrimination in their households and communities. For many, the opportunity to gain employment in the cash economy simply meant more work, since few men were prepared to perform domestic labor.

Reconstituting His Family

On September 7, 1975, following a short but discreet romance, Samora married Graça Simbine. They had moved in similar circles in the colonial capital but had never socialized. They reconnected in 1974 when Graça came to Dar and joined the liberation movement.

After Graça's appointment as minister of education, they worked hard to keep their personal and governmental relationships separate, although Graça told us with a gleam in her eye that "pillow talk" went in many different directions. While Samora rarely discussed their relationship, in her personal correspondence she often addressed him as "Cheri" and ended with such heartfelt salutations as "I live for your love and our family."[52]

Forging a blended family was a challenge. The children, born from three different mothers, were unfamiliar with each other. For more than a decade, only Samito had had contact with their father. Given Samora's patriarchal tendencies, the emotional cost of his lengthy separation from his children, and his emphasis on the importance of family, it's not surprising that he acted decisively, if insensitively, to bring them all to Maputo. Graça remembered that "he was insistent that all the children live together under one roof," despite her reservations about separating them from their mothers. They both rejected a Frelimo proposal that the children live nearby and only eat with them.[53] The transition did not go smoothly. While Irene Buque consented, Sorita Chiankomo and her relatives refused to be separated from her children. Samora ignored their wishes, ordering that the children be brought immediately to the presidential palace.[54]

Despite the demands on him as head of state, Samora devoted time and emotional energy to his children, although it was Graça who oversaw their daily lives while serving as minister of education. In interviews we conducted with four of his children, Olívia, Jucelina, Ornila, and Samito, they described Samora as both a tough disciplinarian and a loving parent who, whenever in Maputo, carved out time to spend with them.[55] During one of these discussions Olívia recalled:

> Our father insisted that we all have dinner at seven o'clock. Nothing could get in the way. Around the

table he and Graça would question us about how our day went and if we had any problems. We often discussed the current situation not only in Mozambique but around the world. He also loved to discuss our family history and could recite events going back nine generations. If one of us did not get a chance to talk, our sibling would insist on having a turn.[56]

Samora also addressed specific problems each of the children faced. Olívia remembered that "he had a lot of patience with me, because, when I arrived at the presidential residence, I could only speak Ronga. He encouraged me when I struggled with Portuguese in special classes that Graça had arranged for me."[57] This concern and compassion extended to all the children. "Although they came from different mothers, he treated them all the same—regardless of parentage and gender."[58]

Samora's insistence that dinner be served promptly was part of the discipline he tried to instill. Both Graça and Olívia described having to rise by 5:30 a.m. to exercise for an hour before breakfast. After school they were expected to complete their homework and exercise at the nearby gym before dinner. Weekends were somewhat less regimented and, when time permitted, Samora would spend part of them playing with the children. Given his competitive nature, he enjoyed challenging them in swimming or running—most often winning until Jucelina and Edelson, another of Samora's sons, became accomplished athletes.[59]

For all his warmth and patience, Samora reacted sternly when his children behaved inappropriately or abused their family position. When Ornila became pregnant as a teenager, he was furious. Apart from the family difficulties it created, she had violated Samora's pronouncements against birth out of wedlock. After a long conversation with her and a family meeting, he publicly announced that she and the father had been sent to a reeducation camp in Niassa. Similarly, when Edelson was sixteen he went to an international trade show and was given a motorcycle he had admired there. After his return he initially lied, claiming it was an unsolicited gift, but ultimately admitted the truth. Samora ordered Edelson to return the motorcycle and warned him that next time he would be severely punished. When Edelson next acted inappropriately, Samora sent him into the army—under a false name, so he would not receive special treatment.[60]

Samora's notion of family extended beyond blood relatives to include many of his closest comrades and their offspring. Nyeleti Mondlane, Eduardo Mondlane's daughter, visited the presidential residence for substantial periods of time. In many of her letters to Graça and Samora, she addressed them as "Dear Parents" and shared intimate details of her life and thoughts.[61] Samora and Graça watched over Nyeleti and her siblings as if they were their own children. Ilundi dos Santos, daughter of Marcelino, along with the offspring of Aquino de Bragança and Joaquim Chissano, had a special place in the hearts of Graça and Samora and spent many hours in the Machel household. On weekends the family often lunched with Jorge and Pamela Rebelo or other old comrades. They celebrated the birthdays and weddings of militants and their children, and Armando Guebuza and Alberto Chipande were asked to "give away" two of Samora's daughters at their weddings.

Being part of Samora's familial network had obvious advantages, but also came with a cost. When Allen asked longtime freedom fighter General Hama Thay to describe Samora's principal shortcoming, he replied without hesitation that "Samora regularly intervened in the private lives of those around him. He was quick to give unsolicited advice and ordered subordinates to cease being womanizers and either act more responsibly or marry their partners."[62] Teodato Hunguana, who had been removed as justice minister, noted that "as a person, Samora cared a great deal about these relationships, but as a president he could be very harsh."[63]

Samora Machel's Marxism and the Defense of the Revolution, 1977–82

The year 1977 marked a turning point. At the Third Party Congress, Frelimo transformed itself from a mass organization committed to People's Power to a Marxist-Leninist party serving the class interests of workers and peasants. For the educational sector, this ideological shift meant little, since the state had already assumed responsibility for primary and secondary education. In the economic sector, by contrast, the new policies generated far-reaching structural changes. Formal recognition of socialist countries as the new nation's "natural allies" also followed.

Mozambique's embrace of Marxism provided justification for Rhodesia and South Africa to intensify their attacks since a Marxist state governed by a revolutionary tied to the Socialist Bloc posed a much greater threat than a merely independent African country. For the West, Frelimo's decision was a major setback in the Cold War.

Moving toward Socialism

The first Mozambican leader to utter the term "socialism" publicly was Samora's mentor, Eduardo Mondlane.

Given the practice of collective self-education in which the leadership typically engaged, it is hardly surprising that Samora's thinking evolved in similar ways. Long before the Third Party Congress, he had begun to embrace the Marxist critique of colonial capitalism. At the time, though, he was more concerned with figuring out how best to prosecute the war than with whether Frelimo should remain a front or become a vanguard revolutionary party. On the eve of independence, Samora had still not decided whether such a transformation made sense in Mozambique. In a 1974 paper presented to policymakers and academics in Moscow, he explained that "the absence of a vanguard party . . . is the result of a web of historical circumstances we face, with characteristics including basically the non-existence of an organized working class and tradition, the lack of struggle experience by the broad masses . . . [and] the isolation of communities, particularly in the countryside."[1]

Nor had Frelimo itself made this determination. Some militants held that Frelimo should continue as a front for the foreseeable future, pointing to the Sandinistas in Nicaragua who had maintained space in their revolutionary party for different progressive tendencies. Aquino de Bragança, an adviser to Samora, warned that becoming a vanguard party would stifle dissent and create an unnecessary link to unpopular and inhumane regimes, such as that of Kim Il-Sung in North Korea. He proposed instead that Frelimo adopt a more generalized socialist project he called "Samorismo," rooted in the new Mozambican reality.[2]

Most senior figures around Samora, however, including Marcelino dos Santos, Sérgio Vieira, Jorge Rebelo,

Oscar Monteiro, and cadres trained in the Soviet Union and China, disagreed. They rejected both Aquino's critique and that of their longtime ally Julius Nyerere. They maintained that Nyerere's notion that precolonial African societies were organized around socialistic principles was an overly romantic reading of the past, one that could neither support radical transformation nor protect Mozambique from counterrevolutionary threats.[3] Support from the socialist camp during the armed struggle and a belief that the defeat of the United States in Vietnam had shifted the global balance of power strengthened their argument. It had also become clear that continued military and economic aid from the Soviet Bloc was predicated on adopting a Marxist line.

By 1976, Samora had concluded that Marxism offered the best path forward. The West's continued antipathy, his romantic view of life in the Soviet Bloc, and the high regard he held for Fidel Castro reinforced his leanings.[4] That said, he was neither pro-Soviet nor pro-Chinese, but committed instead to forging a socialist society born out of Mozambique's experiences. As his old friend José Cabaço recalled, "Samora's socialism came from his visceral reaction to the abuses of colonial capitalism."[5]

Frelimo's debate about the best way forward occurred behind closed doors, making it impossible to discern how the actual process unfolded. Oscar Monteiro, then minister of state apparatus, provides a summary.

> In February 1976, at the end of the 8th Central
> Committee meeting, Samora made a speech calling
> for Frelimo to create a vanguard party. To everyone's
> surprise, I, rather than Armanda Guebuza [the

national political commissar], was assigned the task of preparing the planning documents for the Third Party Congress. There were several others with whom I worked, including [Fernando] Ganhão and Luís [Bernardo Honwana]. We presented two options to the Political Military Committee, whose members included Samora, Marcelino, Chissano, Chipande, and Guebuza. The first option was to create a highly disciplined Marxist-Leninist party based on a Soviet model, capable of mobilizing the people against internal class enemies and external threats. The other alternative rested on the proposition that classes were not yet clearly defined and that Frelimo lacked strong support throughout the country, making it necessary to think of *democracia nova*—something like the Chinese used to mobilize the peasantry.[6]

The leadership unanimously voted for the former.[7] A year later, at the Third Party Congress Samora chaired, the delegates affirmed this position.[8]

While adhering to an orthodox Marxian formulation that the industrial working class is the leading force in forging a socialist society, the congress also departed from it and elevated the role of the peasantry because, during the armed struggle, it "had already presented great proof of its engagement in the revolutionary transformation of our society." In this language one can hear Samora's long-standing appreciation of peasants' political agency. The congress agreed that Frelimo would become a vanguard party whose "historic mission is to lead, organize and educate the masses, thus transforming the popular class movements into a powerful instrument for the destruction of capitalism and the construction of socialism."[9]

During a long interview with Allen Isaacman and Iain Christie two years later, Samora insisted on Marxism's relevance for Mozambique.

> I am going to prove to you, Isaacman, so that you can tell your colleagues [how] peasants and workers, who cannot read or write, come to understand Marxism-Leninism.... Illiterate peasants learned the essence of the system of exploitation of men by men from a new group of exploiters, represented by [Uria] Simango and Lazaro [Nkavandame], who wanted to introduce exploitation into the liberated zones. It was not a Marxist who went to tell them what exploitation was, they did not read it in any book. But they felt the exploitation and knew their exploiters.... They were the ones who fought and made the exploited succeed against the exploitative merchants and landowners.... Marxism-Leninism does not come to our country as an imported product. Hear this very well, this is the idea we want to fight against.... Our party is not a group of intellectuals reading and interpreting Marx, Engels, and Lenin.[10]

While Samora's claim that exploited peasants would necessarily gravitate to Marxism is problematic, his deep respect for many aspects of rural life was clear during this interview.

The Third Party Congress adopted plans to revitalize agriculture and industry along socialist lines. In this report to the congress, Samora sketched out the broad outlines of the new master plan: "Our strategy for development rests on agricultural production. The communal villages are the fundamental lever for liberating the people in the rural areas. Industry is the dynamizing factor for economic development. The building of Socialism demands that the economy be centrally planned and directed by the State."[11]

At the center of rural transformation was the dramatic expansion of communal villages. Samora confidently predicted communal villages would stimulate the agricultural sector and create the opportunity for "a new style of life."[12] Communal village life would be the crucible for the creation of the rural version of the New Man.

Communal villages with their associated agricultural cooperatives appeared to have much to offer. Their location near roads and markets would give them access to services—schools, clinics, storage facilities for crops, and consumer and craft cooperatives—absent in much of the countryside. Ideally, communal villages would be located in fertile zones on carefully laid-out grids with proper housing and sanitation. Collective life and collective production would also enhance the revolutionary consciousness of the peasantry.[13]

It was Frelimo's task to convince peasants, through collective discussions in every locality, to leave their scattered homesteads and move into these large communities. At the end of 1977, there were around a hundred communal villages, including those established during the armed struggle or right after independence, ranging in size from the fifty families at Makonde in Niassa Province to more than eleven thousand families at Julius Nyerere in Gaza. Two years later, over a million peasants were living in communal villages; by

1981, there were 1.2 million—almost 15 percent of the population. In Cabo Delgado more than 90 percent of peasants and refugees returning from Tanzania were resettled in communal villages. In Gaza, with the second-largest number of communal villages, 30 percent were living communally. In no other province did the number exceed 20 percent.[14] One of the most successful was Communal Village 24 de Julio near Xai-Xai in Gaza, close to Samora's home, which was established by local officials working with peasants displaced by floods.[15]

Problems surfaced almost immediately. Planners in the Ministry of Agriculture underestimated the effects of relocation on displaced communities, which lost control over where and how to live as well as access to critical economic and cultural resources. For many, the move also disconnected them from the spirits of ancestors who protected their communities and guaranteed the fertility of women, land, and cattle. Despite their alleged expertise, state planners were often ignorant of the most suitable locations for agriculture and cattle grazing. The government failed to provide peasants with the technical support, seeds, equipment, and consumer goods necessary to make their villages self-sustaining.[16] When productivity declined, officials blamed it on the peasants' inefficient practices, unwillingness to innovate, and lack of motivation, rather than on the government's own failures—all echoes from the colonial past.

Specific local and regional factors also eroded peasant support for communal life. In Nampula Province, party officials aligned with unpopular local chiefs to promote this experiment.[17] Peasants relocating from coastal areas of Cabo Delgado, Inhambane, and Gaza lost their profitable cashew trees without compensation. Moreover, as the war with RENAMO intensified, some provincial governors herded peasants into villages to separate them from the insurgents, leading critics to liken them to the colonial *aldeamentos*.[18]

Peasants increasingly defied state planners, much as they had colonial ones. In Zambézia and Nampula, the two most populous provinces, only 6 percent of the peasant population agreed to join communal villages.[19] Those living in communal villages would work their own fields rather than the collective ones. By 1982, only one-sixth of the communal villages had functioning agricultural cooperatives, and even their most politically motivated members spent only a few hours working in the collective fields.[20] Many men chose to work on state farms rather than in unprofitable communal fields because that was the only way to support their families. Other dissatisfied communal village members simply disappeared.

The government's allocation of most of its limited resources to state farms further undermined the viability of communal villages. Immediately after the Third Party Congress, the Ministry of Agriculture allocated state farms $40 million for heavy equipment, such as tractors, combines, and irrigation pumps, rather than providing peasants with necessary technical inputs. The following year, two-thirds of the agricultural budget went to heavy equipment for state farms.[21]

By allocating scarce resources in this manner, Samora and his advisers were succumbing to the logic of high socialist modernism. Without economies of scale, without agroecological knowledge, even without providing for trained mechanics and spare parts, they believed that simply introducing advanced agricultural technology would by itself increase Mozambique's food security, expand agricultural exports, and provide raw material for its nascent industries. Samora also anticipated that state farms would employ the 150,000 to 200,000 rural workers idled when settlers and foreign companies abandoned their holdings, and that these workers would forge a new class consciousness by laboring together free from colonial exploitation.[22] His conclusions were based on optimistic projections from the Ministry of Planning, directed by Marcelino dos Santos and filled with East German technocrats with no knowledge of the complex and varied agroeconomic and social conditions on the ground.

Although this policy cut rural unemployment and generated modest gains in agricultural production, the state farms failed dismally. Despite receiving the lion's share of the agricultural budget, by 1982 they only accounted for 20 percent of output and none turned a profit. Poor planning, lack of management skills, the limited and largely unhelpful expertise of foreign advisers, failure to maintain equipment, inability to mobilize workers, and low wages that forced farms to rely on seasonal labor doomed the experiment. Nowhere was this clearer than in the fertile Limpopo Valley, where peasants were not prepared to work for low wages as agricultural laborers when they could earn more in the South African mines.[23]

The scale and pace of state control of the industrial sector meanwhile increased dramatically after the Third Party Congress. Planners emphasized heavy industry and large development projects requiring trained workers and substantial investment. Initially, Samora sought assistance from the Socialist Bloc. Ten thousand Mozambicans were sent to East Germany for training beginning in 1979.[24] Samora believed that having Mozambican workers from different regions and social backgrounds living and working side by side in socialist countries would cement their sense of identity as Mozambicans, national pride, and working-class consciousness.[25]

Efforts to revitalize and restructure the industrial sector brought mixed results. Between 1977 and 1981 the economy experienced a modest recovery.[26] By 1979 more than 150,000 industrial workers were again employed fulltime, and absenteeism had dropped by 20 percent.[27] Several industrial projects were completed, including two textile mills, a fish-processing complex, and a joint-venture tire factory funded by American capital. Salaries and working conditions improved in some existing and new factories.[28] Samora felt so confident that he declared Mozambique would solve underdevelopment in the 1980s.[29]

His optimism was misplaced. Despite massive state intervention, by 1980 the economy was in a downward spiral. According to Prakash Ratilal, governor of the central bank during most of this period, a combination of international and domestic factors precipitated the decline, and promised assistance from Western countries was too limiterd to have any significant impact.[30] In the international arena, Mozambique's decision in 1976 to enforce United Nations sanctions against Rhodesia by closing its port at Beira to the settler regime cost the young nation dearly. The following year, South Africa abrogated its agreement to continue the colonial practice of paying the government's wage remittances for migrant laborers in gold at prices well below the world market. Pretoria also reduced its use of the port of Maputo from six million tons before independence to half that figure in 1981. Two years later it capped the number of migrant Mozambican miners at 41,000 rather than 110,000. The steep jump in oil prices with the 1979 Iran-Iraq War also had a devastating effect. Recurring floods, droughts, and cyclones disrupted agricultural production, as did crippling attacks by South African–backed RENAMO terrorists.[31]

As early as 1979, Samora expressed concerns to his economic advisors about the viability of a state-planned economy. After Moscow rebuffed Mozambique's effort to join the Council for Mutual Economic Assistance, the Socialist Bloc's economic union, in 1981 Samora dispatched senior officials to Washington to begin exploratory conversations with the World Bank and the International Monetary Fund. The Soviet Union and East Germany were furious.[32]

By the early 1980s industrial production was still well below preindependence levels. Basic commodities remained in short supply. Almost all factories were still limited to the Maputo-Matola corridor. The socialist countries remained reluctant to provide the necessary capital for large-scale projects. Almost all their aid was tied to disadvantageous barter agreements, in which they exchanged outdated equipment for Mozambique's agricultural exports. In an attempt to jump-start the economy, Samora announced his willingness to seek investment from Western businesses as long as they were "interested in mutually beneficial projects that would ensure an appropriate transfer of technology and guarantee the training of local workers."[33]

Figure 6.1. Lancaster House negotiations: Samora with other Frontline presidents and Zimbabwe leaders Robert Mugabe and Joshua Nkomo. Courtesy of Centro de Documentação Samora Machel (CDSM)

Figure 6.2. Samora greeting African National Congress president Oliver Tambo. Courtesy of Centro de Documentção e Formação Fotográfica (CDFF)

Figure 6.3. Samora and Leonid Brezhnev. (CDFF)

Defending the Revolution:
Combating the Internal Enemy

From the moment Samora assumed the presidency, he feared collaborators and class enemies might subvert the revolution. In a 1977 speech he warned of ominous consequences if Frelimo let down its guard: "Instead of maintaining the offensive, instead of destroying the head of the snake in the egg, if we go back on the defensive, we will discover the snake only when it is fully grown and lifting its venomous head to kill us."[34] These perceived enemies included settlers who longed for a return to white rule, former PIDE officials, Africans who had fought in the colonial army, and covert supporters of rival nationalist organizations. Merchants large and small and religious leaders and churchgoers—especially Jehovah's Witnesses, who refused to recognize the authority of the new government—were also suspect.

Samora also expressed concern about the small but influential urban bourgeoisie, whose lifestyle and values threatened to undermine those the government was trying to instill. The principal culprits were price-gouging merchants and officials who abused their positions to accumulate wealth.

Even more troubling were abuses of power by members of the military or Frelimo cadres. In a 1979 interview with Allen and Iain Christie, Samora described why such abuses of power occurred: "[FRELIMO was] met by godsons of the administrators, godmothers of the [right-wing] national women's movements, members of ANP and of PIDE. They offered cars, houses . . . set up parties and [arranged nice girls] for the FRELIMO commanders."[35] He warned in his Beira speech that corrupt police, security officials (in the Serviço Nacional de Segurança Popular), and party members posed a threat to Mozambique and its citizens and urged the audience to identify and speak out against such traitors.[36]

So obsessed were Samora and his closest colleagues about "covert class enemies" that even clandestine members of the liberation movement who had spent years in colonial jails were not above suspicion. In July 1978, these ex-prisoners were publicly interrogated to determine if any had betrayed the revolution while incarcerated. Samora himself chaired the proceedings. Most were exonerated.[37]

There was particular concern about the more than ninety thousand Africans who had served in the colonial army or secret police, which itself made them "compromised" (*comprometidos*) in Frelimo's eyes.[38] After independence they were disarmed and most were allowed to return home—but in November 1978 Samora ordered that they come forward and acknowledge their collaboration with the colonial regime, after which their pictures were displayed at their workplaces. Samora attended the public meetings, where he ridiculed the comprometidos, called some out by name, and demanded that others perform acts of contrition. Many who denied their complicity were incarcerated without trial. Others were sent to the army.[39] For four years, the comprometidos remained social outcasts. Only in 1982 were those who had acknowledged their misdeeds exonerated and their pictures removed from public display.

As economic and military conditions worsened, calls to punish enemies of the revolution grew even louder. The reintroduction of the unpopular death penalty in 1980 was an indication of how far Samora was willing to go to suppress internal opposition.[40] Three years later the death penalty was allowed for those convicted of serious economic crimes such as smuggling. At roughly the same time the parliament passed the "*lei de chicotada*," which reinstituted corporal punishment, including the colonial practice of whipping, for a wide variety of crimes. Many of Frelimo's most loyal supporters were appalled, but only one member of the government, Justice Minister Teodato Hunguana, opposed the policy.

Defending Mozambique's Sovereignty: Regional Alliances, Nonalignment, and Natural Allies

The final communiqué of the Third Party Congress stressed "Mozambique's commitment to strengthening . . . the struggle against colonialism, racism, neo-colonialism and imperialism." Despite its radical tone, the communiqué also expressed a willingness to establish "mutually beneficial relations with all states, regardless of their social and economic systems."[41]

In order to defend Mozambique's territorial integrity and protect the revolution, the highest priorities were to strengthen relations with the other Frontline States (then comprising Tanzania, Zambia, Angola, and Botswana), challenge South African and Rhodesian military and economic hegemony, and provide support to the African National Congress and Zimbabwe African National Union. Mozambique joined the Organization of African Unity and the Non-Aligned

Movement, promoting the struggles for liberation not only in southern Africa, but also in the western Sahara and Portugal's Asian colony of East Timor.

Samora and Foreign Minister Joaquim Chissano insisted that nonalignment not be equated with neutrality. Addressing the Summit Conference of Non-Aligned States in Havana in 1979, Samora was unequivocal on this point: "Non-alignment is a specific strategy of our peoples to guarantee independence and peace in the face of the cold war imposed by imperialism. . . . Non-alignment is an anti-imperialist strategy for the total liberation of our people." He went on to stress that "it is precisely with the appearance of socialist countries that the correlation of force changed in our favor. . . . The socialist countries are natural allies of our peoples."[42] He rejected efforts by more moderate members to make the Non-Aligned Movement an autonomous third bloc, independent of the superpowers.

Western analysts portrayed Mozambique as a Soviet satellite, ignoring contrary evidence. The staunchly pro-Moscow Marcelino dos Santos insisted to Allen in 1977 that Frelimo had not fought for freedom for fifteen years "to become the pawn of yet another foreign power."[43] His position was similar to what Samora had maintained at the 1976 meeting of nonaligned nations in Sri Lanka, where he strenuously opposed the presence of foreign warships in the Indian Ocean and the circulation or storage of nuclear weapons there. Chissano was even more adamant on this point: "If the United States and the Soviet Union want to fight, they can fight in their own house."[44] To the dismay of Moscow, Samora refused to provide a strategic naval base at one of its ports. He rejected stationing Cuban forces in Mozambique to protect it from Rhodesian and South African aggression, fearing that a Cuban military presence would embroil Mozambique in the Cold War.

Tensions also surfaced around Moscow's "socialist paternalism." Samora privately acknowledged his anger when the Soviets rejected a request to build a steel mill in Mozambique, insisting that such a project was inappropriate given its level of development. The reluctance of Eastern European ideologues to recognize Mozambique as a legitimate socialist country inspired Samora's acerbic comment that "some people seem to think that the development of Marxism ended in October 1917."[45]

Even American diplomats came to realize the paramountcy of Samora's commitment to maintaining Mozambique's sovereignty. Frank Wisner, a senior State Department official who more than once butted heads with the Mozambican leader, acknowledged after his death that "I always knew that he embodied the hopes and aspirations of the Mozambican people for independence, peace and prosperity."[46]

Samora saw no inconsistency between defining the Socialist Bloc as "natural allies" and maintaining a warm relationship with the Scandinavian countries. Norway and Sweden, in particular, had aided FRELIMO during the armed struggle and continued to provide significant material and diplomatic support after independence.

When it was in Mozambique's interest, Samora even reached out to Western countries that had supported Portuguese colonialism. The clearest example was Mozambique's critical role in the 1979 Lancaster House negotiations that led to the independence of Zimbabwe.

Through these deliberations Mozambique scored a double victory. Rhodesia and the military threat it posed to Mozambique were gone forever, and the negotiations raised Samora's stature as a statesman, with the United Kingdom's influential leader Margaret Thatcher hailing him as a man of peace. She subsequently facilitated Mozambique's opening to the West.

Defending the Nation against South African Destabilization

The Rhodesian and South African–backed Mozambique National Resistance was originally composed of remnants of the colonial opposition to FRELIMO and disaffected or expelled FRELIMO guerrillas. Shortly after independence, it adopted a Portuguese name, Resistência Nacional Moçambicana (RENAMO), and Rhodesian security appointed former FRELIMO members André Matsangaissa and Afónso Dhlakama to senior leadership positions in order to create the appearance of legitimacy.[47]

RENAMO unleashed a campaign of fear and terror, torturing and maiming unarmed peasants, press-ganging women and children, burning down rural communities, plundering communal villages, destroying schools and clinics, and sabotaging railroad lines and electrical pylons.[48] Vernácio Leone, who lived in a colonial aldeamento, recounts that "when RENAMO would enter a village, they would call all the people together. Then, they would go into our huts and steal all that was inside. They forced the people back into their homes, which they set on fire."[49] Such violence, including forcing children to cut off the ears or breasts of their mothers to make the children pariahs with no alternative but to join the terrorists, was a central feature of RENAMO strategy—as several interviewees who fled RENAMO as young boys and later asked to remain anonymous described to Allen.[50] According to Stephen A. Emerson, a military historian and former civilian analyst for the US Department of Defense, the "use of terror to intimidate their enemies and ensure support among wavering peasant populations is well-documented in anecdotal accounts, refugee interviews, and multiple postwar studies on the use of violence during the conflict."[51]

Samora and his advisers underestimated the destructive capacity of RENAMO, which they dismissed as a group of "armed bandits," and misjudged the critical role it would play in Pretoria's destabilization campaign. Mozambique's military leadership believed instead that a full-scale invasion from Rhodesia and South Africa was more likely. According to their thinking, a conventional army backed by Soviet-supplied jets, helicopters, tanks, and artillery would best defend against this likelihood. As a result, Mozambique's relatively effective guerrilla force was transformed into an inexperienced, ill-equipped, and poorly led army unable to contain mobile RENAMO bands operating in the countryside.

The assumption that RENAMO would collapse with the fall of the Rhodesian government was another strategic error. Instead, it found a new patron when the South African army transferred RENAMO headquarters and bases to Phalaborwa in the Transvaal. The South African Special Forces Brigade reorganized RENAMO's command structure, trained recruits, planned major operations, and resupplied RENAMO through airdrops and naval landings.[52]

In private, Samora acknowledged that his military was unprepared for RENAMO's resurrection. He sent several elite platoons to the Soviet Union for antiguerrilla training and even recruited African former soldiers who had been part of the Portuguese army's elite counterinsurgency force.[53] It was, however, too little, too late.

By 1982, RENAMO was causing havoc in the countryside. Destruction for destruction's sake was taking its toll. The size of its force had increased from several hundred to several thousand, mostly through coerced recruitment, according to State Department findings.[54] At the same time, Frelimo's tendency to denigrate many aspects of traditional culture as reactionary or obscurantist, its removal of local chiefs, disdain for all religions, and unpopular communal village campaign were alienating many peasants. Savvy RENAMO commanders used this to garner local support in parts of Manica, Sofala, Zambézia, and Nampula by calling for a return to "authentic" African society.[55] Mozambique's experiment was in serious trouble.

The Unraveling of Mozambique's Socialist Revolution, 1983–86

By Samora's eighth year as president, many Mozambicans had become exhausted and disillusioned. The military could not protect citizens, declining economic production was exacerbated by RENAMO attacks, and there were food shortages everywhere. The common refrain, "before, we had colonialism and potatoes, now we have independence and no potatoes," captured the growing sense of despair.

Because Frelimo's Marxist strategy no longer seemed able to solve the growing crises, Samora pushed the leadership to critically assess the assumptions underlying its plans for Mozambique's future. Three seemingly unrelated but inextricably interconnected policies emerged:

- the retreat from socialism announced at the 1983 Fourth Party Congress;

- Operação Produção, a massive relocation to the countryside of the urban unemployed and participants in the informal economy; and

- the Nkomati Accord with South Africa's apartheid regime.

Coming within a year of each other, they shook the revolution to its core.

The Retreat from Socialism

In the last months of 1982, Samora and his comrades took steps they hoped would reverse the party's declining popularity. After high-profile meetings with religious leaders, the government returned some previously nationalized Catholic Church property, created a Department of Religious Affairs inside the Ministry of Justice, and recognized Christmas Day as a national holiday—euphemistically named "Family Day." Samora ordered the pardoning of more than a thousand reputed collaborators and jettisoned the most strident Marxist rhetoric, including such terms as "class enemy" and "vanguardism," in favor of language that instead emphasized patriotism and nationalism.[1] He even rehabilitated several precolonial African rulers—most notably the Shangaan king Ngungunyane, whose bones Samora personally brought back from Lisbon—all of whom had previously been labelled "feudal lords."

None of these gestures addressed the severe economic effects of a mismanaged state economy. Despite heavy investments in sugar, cotton, and other cash crops, output had plummeted, depriving Mozambique of millions of dollars in hard currency. Many state-run farms and industries collapsed, putting thousands of employees out of work. At the same time, the need to import more food and consumer goods intensified the country's severe balance of payment crisis and forced the government to negotiate food aid from whatever sources it could find. The fact that the minister of finance and the governor of the central bank met weekly to determine such questions as whether to import food or medication indicates the severity of the crisis.[2]

Frelimo publicly blamed Mozambique's economic plight on South Africa's destabilization campaign, whose damage was estimated to be as high as $55 billion. In private, however, Samora and some of his closest advisers came to the conclusion that the command economy was also part of the problem.[3] As early as 1980, he announced that the state would no longer be in the business of selling matches and beer, which was better left to private merchants. He also began meeting with Western investors to promote joint economic ventures.

It was not until the Fourth Party Congress in April 1983 that far-reaching economic reforms were proposed and ratified. A report from the Commission for Economic and Social Directives reaffirmed Frelimo's commitment to develop "the bases of a socialist economy," but suggested "radical changes in the structure of the economy." For the first time, the commission recognized the critical role of family-based production and the need for increased state aid, calling for investment in agricultural equipment for the private peasant sector and technical support for organizing a "restructured rural marketing system" to stimulate exchanges.[4] Samora's selection of João Ferreira, an advocate of state funding for peasant initiatives, as minister of agriculture was the clearest indication that practical considerations now overrode ideological concerns.[5]

The report's other radical proposals included calls to achieve greater coordination between private and state companies, "integrate private companies into the

planning system," and "encourage foreign capital investments." Until then, the most significant deviation from
Marxism-Leninism had been Samora's 1981 authoriza-
tion of exploratory talks with the World Bank and the
International Monetary Fund, which broke down when
they demanded that Mozambique end food subsidies
and radically reduce social expenditures. To carry out
these policies, Mozambique needed to adopt technology
appropriately, "ensuring that our tractor driver is able to
understand the machine and keep it in operation."[6] At
a rally shortly after the congress, Samora acknowledged
that Frelimo had "erroneously developed a hostile attitude to private enterprise that must be changed."[7]

The mandates of the Fourth Party Congress and
resulting government policies were somewhat contradictory. While continuing to follow a socialist master
plan, Samora's administration "responded to pressure
from below by relaxing restrictions on trade, working
together with private companies, or allocating land
to smallholders."[8] It discarded fixed salaries in state-
owned industries, allowing managers to set wages
based on productivity. It contracted with foreign firms
to restore the country's transportation network and
Cahora Bassa's power lines, both severely damaged by
RENAMO. Long-term loans from France and Italy to-
taling more than $300 million and an economic accord
with Brazil were the first major commercial agreements
with Western countries outside Scandinavia.

Several of the most dogmatic ideologues vehemently
opposed this retreat from Marxism. Samora countered
that he was not abandoning socialist ideals, but seeking "a socialism that would work in Mozambique." He

172

reaffirmed this position in a *60 Minutes* interview on American television. When asked whether he was a communist, he responded, "I want to feed my people, I want to dress my people, I want wealth to go to my people. If that means that I am a communist, then I am a communist."[9]

Operação Produção

Unlike responses to pressures from below, Operação Produção—"Operation Production," a project to make urban citizens "economically productive"—was an example of Samora's and Frelimo's slide toward authoritarianism. Even as the state loosened its control over the economy, it tightened the regulation of city dwellers. These two seemingly contradictory policies were, in fact, connected.

Mozambique's economic decline had precipitated the migration of thousands to the major urban centers in search of employment and a better life. The additional influx of refugees fleeing RENAMO and recently fired mineworkers returning from South Africa compounded economic and social problems in Maputo and elsewhere. Between 1973 and 1978, Maputo's population almost doubled, and it continued increasing at a rapid rate. This infusion strained housing, food supplies, and health care.[10]

Much has been written about abuses associated with the "cleansing" of the cities, which Frelimo had unsuccessfully attempted several times. Its leaders, many of whom had spent more than a decade in the bush, never fully comprehended the complexities of urban life or the vibrancy of its informal economy, particularly in the shantytowns. At independence, the Frelimo leadership was surprised that Maputo and Beira suffered from rampant crime, widespread violence, extensive drug networks, and gangs of robbers and racketeers. Samora insisted that there were "tens of thousands of prostitutes in the big cities at the time of our independence."[11] He attributed this moral decay to the bourgeoisie—both black and white—who continued to hold a grip on urban life.[12] In response, he became the moral guardian of the nation, specifying appropriate comportment for the "masses" and defining the enemy "according to a taxonomy of moral failings—laziness, corruption and self-indulgence."[13]

Seven years of Frelimo rule had not eliminated these activities. Arresting prostitutes, drug dealers, smugglers, black marketeers, petty criminals, and malingerers had no significant impact.[14] The continued homelessness, hunger, unemployment, and crime was an affront to Samora's dream of creating the New Man. To tackle these problems and more effectively control the urban population, a radical moral and political intervention was needed. To Samora and the Frelimo leadership, the issuance of residence cards was the appropriate solution.

In 1982, the government began distributing residence cards to every worker with a recognized job as proof of urban citizenship. These cards had to be shown to access basic social services ranging from housing and health care to food rations and transport. According to Teodato Hunguana, "most urban residents approved of the cards, seeing them as an effective form of population control that would reduce vagrancy."[15]

Their introduction, however, did not solve the problems facing urban areas. The continued influx of migrants and increasing unemployment convinced Samora that the only alternative to urban decay was a radical purge of "unproductive" citizens from the cities. The plan under Operation Production was to relocate them to faraway, underpopulated Niassa Province, whose fertile land would easily support them.

At the Fourth Party Congress there was general consensus that "the cities were overcrowded with idle rural migrants who made it difficult for the working people to have enough food, housing and all the other benefits of citizenship."[16] Addressing a rally on May 21, 1983, Samora declared that "only those who have work, who have waged work, are entitled to residence [in the city]. . . . The marginals, the unemployed, the vagrants should be sent to the countryside, to production."[17]

Samora selected Minister of the Interior Armando Guebuza to oversee this urban cleansing. Guebuza had played a similar role in a previous unsuccessful attempt by Frelimo to rid Maputo of undesirables and "wicked women." So began the much-hated Operation Production, which was initially voluntary. The unemployed were asked to register and encouraged to relocate outside the cities. When few actually did, expulsion quickly became compulsory.

The most basic problem with Operation Production was the complete lack of knowledge about informal-sector employment. The absence of agreed definitions of "vagabonds" and "socially marginal" persons was a related obstacle. For the Frelimo leadership, those working in the informal sector, such as petty traders, handymen, artisans, barbers and beauticians, reed-house builders, and others who were self-employed, did not count as "real" workers and were lumped together as potential Xiconhocas.

The campaign began in June 1983 and ended in May 1984. In less than a year, approximately one hundred thousand citizens were arbitrarily rounded up and sent to Niassa, the most remote and least developed province in the country. Almost half came from Maputo, but thousands were also expelled from Beira, Nampula, and other urban centers. Single women, already suspect, were particularly vulnerable, since they were less likely to have registration papers. Most of the displaced were sent directly to reeducation camps, although several hundred more fortunate souls went to the state farm at Unango to work as paid laborers.[18]

The entire process suffered from "unruliness and gross violations of the most basic civil rights."[19] Overworked judges, under pressure from local party officials, rarely investigated whether those detained were actually in the cities illegally. State officials and even ordinary citizens sometimes used Operation Production as a way to settle old scores.

The rural reeducation centers bore little relationship to those established by FRELIMO during the armed struggle, which had been designed to wipe out corrupt tendencies and instill revolutionary values.[20] There were few classes and the camp commanders themselves, many of whom had fought in the armed struggle, rarely had more than rudimentary educations. Detainees spent their time working in the gardens, building and repairing thatch huts, or merely sitting. To escape boredom, many smoked *dagga* (marijuana), which was easily accessible. Thus, the "socially marginal" detainees, discarded and forgotten by all but their families and close friends, derived nothing beneficial from being sent there.

The reeducation camps did not resemble Soviet Gulags, as Samora's critics claimed.[21] Benedito Machava, in a scathing indictment of Frelimo's reeducation camps, is clear on this point: "The iconic elements of internment camps—barbed wires, watch towers, and armies of well-equipped security forces—were absent from Mozambique's camps. Reeducation camps had no fence, no watch tower, and few armed guards. Authorities assumed that the remote location of the camps . . . was enough to curb escapes."[22] Our brief 1984 visit to a reeducation center in Niassa supports Machava's contention.

Concerns about conditions in the camps, raised by Mozambican visitors living in Niassa, fell on deaf ears. Niassa's governor, Sérgio Vieira, acknowledged the problems in public meetings but insisted that only Guebuza had the authority to make changes.[23] A delegation of concerned citizens actually flew to Maputo to present Guebuza with accounts of the deplorable conditions and even brought photos of dead babies dismembered by lions. After they waited all day to meet with him, he responded coldly, "Don't you think I know this? Go home."[24]

Operation Production was an unmitigated disaster. It failed to alleviate economic and social problems in Mozambican cities, permitted gross abuses, erased important gains in revamping the judicial system, and violated the rule of law. It put a terrible strain on local resources in Niassa and disrupted airline service throughout the country during the four months it took to transport all the "undesirables." There were no plans to return the displaced to their urban homes, and, according to Arlindo Chilundo, Niassa's former governor, thousands of the displaced and their descendants still reside in Niassa today.[25]

Operation Production also seriously damaged Samora's reputation as a man of the people. Teodato Hunguana, minister of justice, had warned him that forced expulsion trampled on the constitutional rights of citizens.[26] Many journalists expressed their outrage and victims and their families wrote directly to Samora about the suffering. In response, Samora effectively ended the program eleven months after it began—although it was not officially abolished until four years later in May 1988.[27]

According to those close to him, Samora was furious when he learned of the abuses. In 1985, a year after ending Operation Production, he expelled Guebuza from the Political Bureau and stripped him of his position as minister of the interior, demoting him to minister without portfolio. Samora also raged that the abuses Guebuza had committed had created additional internal enemies.[28] Only Guebuza's support within the military and state security apparatus and his membership on Frelimo's Political Bureau prevented Samora from removing him entirely from the government.[29]

In addition to the reeducation camps established during Operation Production, Frelimo had been detaining political prisoners since the time of the armed struggle. Among the most significant were Frelimo dissidents Uria Simango and Lazaro Nkavandame, as well as Joanna Simião, who had been a leader of an anti-FRELIMO separatist organization based in Beira.

At independence, all three were being held in a re-education center in northern Mozambique. It was Samora's intention to periodically showcase them to teach future generations about the threats posed by internal enemies.

In areas where Frelimo's policies were most unpopular, particularly Nampula and Zambézia, insurgent commanders were able to rally local communities and chiefs to create a base of supporters. In 1983, after significant RENAMO advances in northern Mozambique, Samora and his military and intelligence advisers feared that, to enhance its claim of being a legitimate nationalist movement, RENAMO soldiers would try to free the three political prisoners. Samora ordered Aurélio Manave, governor of Niassa, to ensure that RENAMO was unsuccessful. Manave, together with senior officials from internal security (Serviço Nacional de Segurança Popular) and military intelligence, executed the "traitors" to make sure they would never fall into RENAMO's hands.[30]

The degree of Samora's involvement remains in dispute. Simango's biographer claims that Samora personally ordered him killed. Fernando Ganhão, Frelimo's official historian, and others close to the Mozambican leaders maintain that Samora had no knowledge of the execution.[31] Ganhão's assertion seems fanciful, since it is highly unlikely that such a significant decision could have been taken without at least Samora's tacit approval.

On the other hand, José Luís Cabaço, minister of information at that time, recently told Allen that when Samora found out, he angrily called the killing of Simango "the height of stupidity."[32] A former journalist who had regular access to the leadership insisted that

Samora only learned of the execution from the Portuguese ambassador, who objected to Manave's proposed appointment as Mozambique's ambassador to Lisbon based on a report by Portuguese intelligence that Manave was involved in Simango's murder.[33] After receiving this information, Samora removed Manave from his position as governor of Niassa.

No matter who actually planned and carried out the killings, Samora, as president, bore ultimate responsibility and his reputation suffered accordingly. Relations with his longtime allies Presidents Nyerere and Kaunda were damaged when they learned Samora had failed to keep the promise he made to them at the time of independence, to protect the three prisoners from harm.

The Nkomati Accord

Despite assistance from Zimbabwe and Tanzania, the military situation continued to deteriorate. Eventually, RENAMO's advance's convinced Samora and his advisers that the war could not be won. They were forced to acknowledge that protecting Mozambique's sovereignty would require both a negotiated settlement with South Africa and elimination of the perception that Mozambique was a pawn of the Soviet Union.

By 1982, Samora had come to realize that the Soviets and their allies were either unwilling or unable to provide the military hardware Mozambique needed. Apart from a handful of MiG-21 jet fighters and Mil Mi-24 helicopter gunships, the heavy weaponry they had received from the Soviets was out of date, costly, and useless against guerrillas. Samora was also rebuffed when he requested assistance in training the larger numbers of counter-insurgency soldiers needed to effectively contain RENAMO. Soviet military officials eventually agreed to take only a small number of officers, who were trained in Siberia, of all places. Moscow's reluctance led Samora to conclude that its principal objective was not to deter RENAMO but to use Mozambique as a pawn in its Cold War struggle against the West. Samora turned to the British and Portuguese, but while they provided counter-insurgency training for Mozambican soldiers, the numbers trained were inadequate.

Samora's plans also met resistance from some senior military commanders who prized their access to heavy weaponry and were committed to conventional warfare. Ignoring his orders, they dispersed members of the newly trained units rather than following Samora's instructions to deploy them together on strategic fronts. It was the first time any generals had disobeyed Samora. It would not be the last.

Samora's unenthusiastic reception in Moscow the following year, while heading a military delegation, solidified his belief that Mozambique was no longer a high priority. Upon his return, disappointed and disillusioned, he confessed to one minister that "we can no longer accept the notion that the Soviet Union is our certain natural ally."[34]

To blunt South African aggression, therefore, Mozambique needed to strengthen its ties to the West. Samora first reached out to British prime minister Margaret Thatcher. She arranged a meeting the following year with her close ally President Ronald Reagan, who Samora endearingly addressed as "Ronnie."[35] Neither provided tangible assistance.

At this point, the only way to end the war was to initiate negotiations with South Africa. Samora brought this plan first to Frelimo's Political Bureau and then to the Council of Ministers. No one appears to have disagreed.

Three of Samora's closest advisors took the lead in negotiating the broad contours of the "Agreement on Non-Aggression and Good-Neighborliness," which came to be known as the Nkomati Accord. Jacinto Veloso, minister of security, was the senior member of the negotiating team. Oscar Monteiro, an attorney and member of the Political Bureau, also played a pivotal role. Fernando Honwana, a rising star in Frelimo who had been Samora's personal representative during the Lancaster House negotiations, was the third key member.

Serious discussions only began in December 1983, although the year before Honwana had held exploratory conversations in Switzerland with RENAMO representatives. Negotiations were long and arduous. The parties recognized, however, that an accord was in both their interests. After difficult discussions punctuated by a South African walkout following Monteiro's denunciation of Pretoria's history of racist aggression, they hammered out the final terms, which included a nonaggression pact and establishment of a joint commission to implement the accord.[36] The final document was signed in a public ceremony in Nkomati, a South African town on the Mozambican border, on March 16, 1984.

Many of Frelimo's allies were infuriated with Samora. They had seen him in military garb speaking civilly with his and their arch-enemy, South African Prime Minister P. W. Botha. They had heard Samora declare that the signing of the agreement was "a high point in the history of relations between our two states and a high point in the history of our region."[37] And they realized that, with this treaty, Frelimo was abandoning its historic commitment to the African National Congress (ANC). President Julius Nyerere of Tanzania, who had been informed of the general terms of the accord before its signing and who privately agreed that Mozambique had no alternative, was publicly furious.[38] The Soviet Union and its allies, the South African Communist Party, and antiapartheid activists across the world condemned the decision as a betrayal of massive proportions. Senior ANC militants, while initially hostile, reluctantly concluded that Mozambique had no other options.

Within some circles in Mozambique there was confusion and anger, especially after Samora claimed Mozambique had forced Pretoria to the bargaining table and that the accord was a great victory for the revolution. Carlos Cardoso, many of his colleagues at the state-run Mozambican Information Agency, and some Eduardo Mondlane University faculty members challenged this representation of the agreement. For them, the Nkomati Accord was an shameful retreat.[39] Rumors began circulating in Maputo that dissatisfied security forces linked to Guebuza were planning a coup.[40]

Under the treaty, South Africa and Mozambique pledged that neither would permit its country to be used by third parties to commit acts of violence against either the territorial integrity or political independence of the other. For South Africa, the accord ensured that Mozambique stopped supporting the ANC and precluded possible attacks by Soviet forces stationed in Mozambique—about which Pretoria was paranoid. In exchange, Mozambique received South Africa's guarantee that it would cease its military assistance to RENAMO.[41] Although South Africa also sought diplomatic recognition and other concessions, Samora refused to budge.

Samora's belief that the Nkomati Accord would provide opportunity for Mozambique to rebuild turned out to be illusory, since Pretoria never ended its military assistance to RENAMO. The South African Defense Force continued to air-drop arms and ammunition, use submarines operating off Mozambique's coast to resupply guerrilla units, and allow large numbers of RENAMO insurgents to cross into Mozambique from their camps in the Transvaal.[42] Documents captured in 1985 at RENAMO headquarters in Gorongoza revealed the extent of the charade.

South African security forces also kept resupplying RENAMO forces based in Malawi, adjacent to the Mozambican border.[43] Anxious to stem this flow of men and arms, Samora flew to Malawi in 1985 in a failed attempt to convince President Hastings Banda to stop supporting RENAMO. Over the next year, several thousand RENAMO terrorists launched major attacks in central Mozambique from their Malawian bases, capturing district capitals and threatening to cut Mozambique in half.[44] RENAMO scored a propaganda victory by claiming that it was now fighting in all ten Mozambican provinces.

It wasn't long before Mozambique was forced to allow inclusion of a RENAMO representative on the accord's monitoring commission, which both legitimated

RENAMO and allowed South Africa to claim the role of peacemaker between two warring Mozambican factions. In October 1985, Mozambique withdrew from the monitoring commission, marking the effective end of the Nkomati Accord.

Still, the accord benefited Mozambique in a number of ways. Although South Africa secretly continued to support RENAMO, the amount of assistance decreased. More importantly, without the accord, covert aid from the United States to South Africa and RENAMO would likely have risen as the Reagan administration intensified its efforts to blunt Soviet influence.

Supporters of the accord also maintained that it paved the way for the 1986 Pretoria meetings, in which RENAMO representatives met with the same Mozambican officials who had negotiated at Nkomati. Several senior Frelimo leaders criticized this meeting because it gave additional credibility to RENAMO.[45] Nonetheless, the discussions were an important first step in the long process toward peace, culminating in the Rome Agreement in 1992.

By 1986, most of Samora's dreams had evaporated. He was becoming increasingly ill-tempered and isolated. Early in the year, the Council of Ministers and the Political Bureau of Frelimo decided to offset Samora's power by creating the new positions of prime minister and president of the Popular Assembly. Although this was presented as an opportunity for Samora to focus on the war against RENAMO, the backstory is more complicated. A group of young Turks, frustrated that their generation had been frozen out of positions of power, allied with at least one senior official to introduce the changes at a meeting of the Central Committee. Samora was startled, but he ultimately agreed and, in a face-saving gesture, publicly announced the changes.[46]

There were additional challenges to his authority. In parliament, Guebuza and supporters criticized Samora's rehabilitation of the Gaza king Ngungunyane, questioning why he had ignored other important rulers with whom he had no ethnic affiliation.[47] Senior military officials disregarded or disobeyed his orders, there were rumors of imminent military coups, and at least of one of his closest comrades privately accused him of acting like a dictator.[48] By negotiating with the apartheid regime, he had irreversibly damaged his position as a revolutionary hero, domestically and internationally.

Samora's personal life suffered as well. His children remember that their fun-loving father became more distant and short-tempered.[49] Life became tense after there was at least one attempt on his life and rumors surfaced about an impending coup.[50] Samora's relationship with Graça, who worked hard to keep the family together, suffered as well. She confided to a friend that "Samora was in a very bad way."[51]

Worst of all, Samora would never live to see his dream of peace in Mozambique realized.

Who Killed Samora?

At approximately nine o'clock on the night of October 19, 1986, the presidential jet carrying Samora and his advisers from Lusaka to Maputo mysteriously smashed into the Lebombo Mountains in South Africa, less than one kilometer from the Mozambican border. Of the thirty-five passengers, all but nine perished—Samora among them.

The next afternoon, after hours of public uncertainty and rumor, Marcelino dos Santos announced, his voice breaking, that Samora was dead. The official declaration from the Popular Assembly, Council of Ministers, and Frelimo Central Committee described his death as an "irreparable loss for the Mozambican people, for Africa, and for humanity."[1]

Mozambicans were in shock. *Tempo*, the nation's leading weekly, was flooded with letters expressing disbelief and sorrow. Many condemned the apartheid regime. One headline read "the Boers killed the best son of the people of Mozambique" while another predicted that "the blood of those who fell will burn apartheid."[2] Typical was the letter from Estêvão Passangeze, who referred to Samora as "our father," a term that many Mozambicans used to describe his special place in their hearts. Estêvão wrote of his fury at the apartheid regime and assured Samora that "you will always be in our souls and together we will continue the Revolution you inspired." Eduardo Mussegula, a high school student in Nampula, echoed this sentiment, predicting that Samora's memory and all he had accomplished "would live on for eternity."[3]

Messages from dignitaries around the world ranging from Fidel Castro to Maureen Reagan, as well as from ordinary foreigners, mourned Samora's loss.[4] Coretta Scott King, in her letter of condolence to Graça Machel, drew parallels between the tragic loss of Samora and her husband's murder: "President Machel possessed exceptional grace and sensitivity. He seemed to perceive things in a fresh light. . . . When I was in his presence, I saw a man who exhibited unsuspected possibilities of purpose and action. Your dear husband lived to see a free and independent People's Republic of Mozambique. Like Martin, he may have not lived long enough to fulfill his own possibilities, but his dream remains for you, your family and his people, who he loved dearly."[5]

Two key South African figures on opposite sides did not attend Samora's funeral. President P. W. Botha's request to participate was vehemently rejected. In disbelief, a high-level official declared, "it is simply unimaginable that Botha come here."[6] From his jail cell on Robben Island, Nelson Mandela pleaded to be allowed to personally honor his fallen comrade. In more than twenty years of incarceration, this was the only time he had asked to be temporarily released. His request fell on deaf ears. In a personal letter to Graça, Winnie Mandela wrote:

> Never before have we made application to leave South Africa. Today we believed that our place was to be with you physically.

Each one of us is imprisoned in different jails. We were prevented from being present with you today to share your sorrow, to weep with you, to lighten your grief, to hold you very close. Our grief for Comrade Samora is so deep that it tears away at the heart. Throughout the night we have kept vigil with you. Throughout today we shall mourn with you for a mighty soldier, a courageous son, and a noble statesman.[7]

In Zimbabwe on the morning of October 20th, an estimated crowd of five thousand stoned the offices of South African Airlines, Malawi Airways, and the American embassy.[8] Citizens throughout South Africa mourned his death in other ways. A young South African film producer said of Samora, "In his military fatigues and AK-47 he was our guerrilla in the bush."[9] From Guinea to Portugal and Mali to Egypt, there were days, even weeks, of national mourning for the "beloved son of Africa who fought against racial discrimination and was a source of inspiration for those in this continent and across the world."[10]

The Prelude to the Crash

After Zimbabwe's independence in 1980, the Malawian government allowed South African military officers to enter the country and provide arms and training to RENAMO forces based there. This assistance continued even after the signing of the Nkomati Accord. On September 11, 1986, Samora flew to Blantyre to meet with President Banda. He provided Banda with documentation of the Malawi–South Africa connection and warned there would be harsh consequences if Malawi's aid to RENAMO continued. The meeting failed to yield any tangible results.

Samora was livid. During an impromptu news conference at the Maputo airport upon his return, he accused the South African military of using Malawian territory to destabilize and destroy Mozambique. When asked what Mozambique would do, he laid out a plan of action: "First, put missiles all along the Malawian border. We've got plenty of missiles, they just don't have a target. Secondly, close Malawi's route through Mozambique to Zimbabwe and South Africa."[11] He then took a highly publicized trip to Tete to assess the preparedness of troops stationed along the Malawian border.[12] Further stoking public outrage, the Mozambican Youth Organization demonstrated outside the Malawian embassy in Maputo. There were protests near the Malawian border in Tete Province, where the participants expressed "rage . . . and frustration with the fact that Malawi was supporting RENAMO's effort to divide Mozambique along the Zambezi."[13] Samora then made another publicized visit to Mozambique's principal air base in Nacala, from which MiGs could easily attack Malawi.

Whether Samora's threats were bluster or not, they clearly concerned Pretoria, which over the next month undertook an intense saber-rattling campaign. Defense Minister Magnus Malan threatened reprisals after a land mine exploded in South Africa, for which it held Mozambique responsible.[14] South African military jets regularly violated Mozambican airspace. Pretoria announced it would no longer allow Mozambican workers in South African mines, costing Mozambique $50 million in hard currency. The state-aligned media began circulating rumors that Samora had lost the confidence of his people and was facing strong opposition within his government.

One account even falsely claimed that Samora had been forced to flee Maputo to nearby Inhaca Island.[15]

Pretoria had many reasons to want Samora dead. He had long been a symbol of opposition to apartheid, capturing the imagination of South Africa's militant youth who adopted the Frelimo slogan, *A luta continua*, as their own. Protestors regularly carried signs celebrating the Mozambican revolution, teenagers sauntered through shantytowns playing rap songs that lionized Samora, and photographs and drawings of him were plastered surreptitiously in public spaces and on abandoned buildings.

On October 11, 1986, the Mozambican government announced that Pretoria was planning to attack Maputo in order to replace Samora with a leader more to its liking. Later that day, Samora met privately with a small group of Mozambican journalists. When Carlos Cardoso expressed his fear that the South African regime was planning to assassinate him, Samora interrupted, declaring, "They've already tried. In November 1985, they infiltrated bazookas into Mozambique that were to have been used to assassinate me." He paused and then declared, "I am in their way, I have not sold out to anyone."[16] Although no independent verification of such an attempt exists, South African hit squads had previously killed African National Congress members in Maputo and there is evidence they were still operating there.[17]

Eight days later, Samora and senior advisors flew to Zambia to meet with President Kaunda and Angola's president José Eduardo dos Santos to explore ways of containing South Africa's regional destabilization efforts.[18] The meeting ended at dusk. Although standing policy prohibited the president from flying at night,

Samora insisted on returning to Maputo that evening so he could attend a meeting the following morning at which he planned to announce sweeping changes to the military leadership. He intended to replace ineffective or compromised senior officials with better-trained younger officers in whom he had greater confidence.

It was not until ten hours after the crash that South African foreign minister Roelof "Pik" Botha informed Sérgio Vieira, Mozambique's interior minister, of the deaths of Samora and most of the others on the plane. In the interim, security forces combed through the wreckage, removing personal belongings and confidential documents. The delegation from Maputo arrived early that afternoon. They found the bodies of the victims covered with sheets and blankets and Samora's remains in a sealed plastic bag inside a coffin. Carlos Cardoso described the moment he saw Samora's corpse: "The bag was opened from the head downwards, but my first strong feeling that I really was looking at the body of Samora Machel came when I saw his right hand, resting on his abdomen. Those hands in life never stopped moving. They are engraved on the memories of many Mozambicans through personal contact with the President, through photographs and films, through the many meetings and rallies he addressed. Only later did I notice a small portion of the beard that become famous across the world."[19]

The Death of Samora: Pointing toward Murder

More than thirty years later, only incomplete evidence has been released about the cause of the crash. Those who planned and carried out the plot to kill Samora remain unidentified despite investigations by the Margo

Commission, established by white-ruled South Africa in 1987; postapartheid South Africa's Truth and Reconciliation Commission, which heard testimony on the crash in 1998; and a joint Mozambican–South African commission established in 2010.

Predictably, South Africa immediately denied any involvement, blaming the "accident" on pilot error. Foreign Minister Botha announced that traces of alcohol had been found in the blood of the Soviet pilots.[20] Rumors circulated that the pilot lacked experience, despite the fact that Captain Yuri Novodran had flown in and out of Maputo more than seventy times, mostly at night.[21] The 1987 Margo Commission also blamed pilot error, but materials that might shed light on its investigation remain under lock and key in South Africa's military and national archives. Eleven years later, Colonel João Honwana, a Mozambican Air Force commander who was an expert witness at the Truth and Reconciliation Commission (TRC) investigation, challenged Pretoria's mischaracterization of the pilot and crew's experience and skill, noting, "I had flown in the very aeroplane with them many times."[22]

The TRC heard other evidence, including from South African military officials, that casts serious doubt on the Margo Commission's findings. Much of the testimony, which has only recently been released, points directly to involvement by the apartheid regime.[23] Certainly, Pretoria had a motive, and it had attempted to assassinate Samora before.[24]

The most probable explanation is that the South Africans had placed a powerful portable navigation beacon near the crash site.[25] Since it transmitted on the same frequency as the VOR beacon at the Maputo airport and used the same code sign, it would have been able to override Mozambique's, which may have been turned off. The pilots were relying on signals they thought were coming from Maputo when, eighty miles from the capital, they were lured off course. Testifying before the TRC, Colonel João Honwana confirmed that, based on the limited evidence Mozambique had "through the flight data and the cockpit voice records, it was clear to us that the crew was convinced that they were following the VOR. The Maputo VOR."[26]

The first inkling of electronic sabotage surfaced the morning after the crash. Sérgio Vieira, who was leading the Mozambican delegation, was inexplicably told by Johan Coetzee, the local South African police commissioner, that "my [helicopter] crew is saying you have to look for a beacon over there [near the crash site]." The following day, a United Press International correspondent reported receiving an anonymous tip from a man claiming to be a South African Air Force officer that the military had placed a decoy beacon near the site.[27] Subsequent review of the transcript from the cockpit's voice recorders revealed the pilot's surprise that the VOR was directing the automatic pilot to fly southwest, rather than remaining on course. He could be heard reporting to the Maputo tower that he could not see the lights of the city.

Pretoria refused to share information with the Mozambican technical and security teams that might have clarified the cause of the crash. Nevertheless, Armando Guebuza, then minister of transportation, who oversaw the Mozambican side of the investigation, expressed confidence that the fragmentary evidence was sufficient to support the conclusion that "the plane was following signals from a VOR which was not the one in Maputo. It was this VOR that caused the plane's fatal turn away from its normal route."[28]

According to Willem Oosthuizen, a member of the South African Security Branch testifying at the TRC, this was not the first time Pretoria had used such a ruse, having deployed portable beacons in Namibia as early as 1979. Even more damaging was his testimony that two weeks after the crash, at a small military intelligence base near the crash site, he observed a cylindrical "movable beacon" about four feet in height with an aerial on top. "When I saw it . . . I realized that it was no accident."[29] Oosthuizen also testified that while subsequently on patrol along the Indian Ocean coast he noticed people on a trawler throwing things overboard, including a cylinder that "looked specifically like the one I had seen a few days earlier at the Security Police" base.[30] Afraid for his life, he had remained silent for more than a decade, until he was threatened with prosecution if he refused to testify.

The TRC also heard from three other South African Defense Force members, all of whom described a beacon they had seen prior to the crash and opined that it could easily have been transported by jeep. Colonel Mossie Basson, an electronics warfare expert, reported that members of the ultra-secret Signals Intelligence Division had been in Mbuzini the night of the crash.[31] Local residents also recalled a temporary military camp at Busoni that was dismantled around that time.[32] Additionally, TRC investigators learned that South African military forces were on full alert the night of the crash and that an elite commando reconnaissance unit had been dispatched to the area where the plane went down.[33] Finally, senior military officials, including Special Forces general Jeep Joubert and Chief of Military Intelligence Kat Liebenberg, reportedly flew into the area and spent the night of the crash at the nearby Spitskop Special Forces base.[34]

There is additional evidence that implicates the apartheid regime. Several days before the crash, South Africa's defense minister Magnus Malan flew secretly to Malawi, where he and his Malawian counterparts discussed the best way to eliminate Samora.[35] A night or two before the crash, Paulo de Oliveira, the RENAMO chief in Lisbon, received urgent instructions from South African security that the insurgents should "claim responsibility for shooting down Samora's plane."[36]

Much of the most damning information was uncovered by TRC researcher Debra Patta. She received anonymous death threats, including one from a caller warning her that if she did not cease her investigation he "would put a gun to her head." On another occasion, she was confronted by individuals who told her that she would "be burned up altogether" if she continued to play with fire.[37]

Within Mozambique, many still believe that disgruntled Mozambican officials played a part in Samora's death. Although they are reluctant to speak on the record for fear of retribution, some insist the crash could not have happened without some Mozambican involvement, pointing to the malfunctioning Maputo airport beacon and erratic radio communications between the tower and the presidential plane.[38] Others stress that Samora had many enemies and that his erratic behavior and declining popularity emboldened his opponents.

Under domestic and international pressure to determine who actually planned Samora's death, Mozambique and the government of postapartheid South Africa formed a bilateral commission in 2010 to do just that. After conducting extensive interviews in Mozambique, South Africa, and neighboring countries, in 2014 the investigators requested a meeting with President Guebuza. It apparently never occurred. The status and substance of whatever report was produced remains unknown, and there is no indication that further investigation was ever undertaken.[39]

8.1 Female soldiers responding to the death of Samora Machel.

The Political Afterlife of Samora and the Politics of Memory

In the last years of his life Samora and the entire Frelimo leadership had been forced to compromise their radical agenda. Mozambique's next president, Joaquim Chissano, who served from 1986 to 2005, went even further, totally abandoning the socialist project in favor of neoliberalism and market capitalism.

As part of the process of repudiating Frelimo's radical past, Mozambique's leaders sought to diminish Samora's significance. Yet this campaign, which M. Ann Pitcher has aptly described as "organized forgetting," did not eradicate the memories of the late president from the hearts and minds of millions of Mozambicans. For many, in death Samora became a romanticized symbol. So powerful was the nostalgia surrounding him that Chissano's successor, Armando Guebuza, who served from 2005 to 2015, reversed course and resurrected Samora's image. He did so to promote his own narrow nationalist agenda, despite the tension that had existed between the two during Samora's life.

Erasing Socialism, Erasing Samora

When Chissano took office, the country was in the throes of multiple crises. The most pressing were the continued economic collapse and the enormous national debt, estimated at over $3 billion. With limited options, Chissano sought relief from the International Monetary Fund and the World Bank. These institutions demanded, as a precondition for extending loans, that the Chissano government adopt a policy of structural adjustment requiring two major concessions: eliminating state subsidies for food, housing, health care, and education and reducing support for other social services; and removing barriers to private foreign investment.

After a brief attempt to commingle socialist ideals with free-market policies, both Chissano's government and Frelimo succumbed to the pressure. At the Fifth Party Congress in 1989, Frelimo formally abandoned Marxist-Leninism, dropping its claim to be a "party of the worker-peasant alliance." Instead, it became a conventionally nationalist "party of all the people" with a free-market agenda.

The 1987 IMF agreement was the death knell of Mozambican socialism. The preamble of the new constitution enacted in 1990, while celebrating the struggle that led to independence, omitted any reference to free health care and education as rights of citizenship. May Day parades became tepid events at which officials simply called for higher wages and limits on inflation. The capitalist entrepreneur replaced the socialist New Man in government publications and investment journals.[1]

Mozambique's relationship with RENAMO was similarly whitewashed. No longer was RENAMO referred to as a group of armed bandits, or even as insurgents. Instead, during peace negotiations that extended from 1990 to 1992, President Chissano embraced them as "our brothers in the bush." The June 1992 treaty signed in Rome under the auspices of the Catholic Church recognized RENAMO as a legitimate party with the right to participate in the political process.

The long, highly contested process of rewriting the national anthem was emblematic of the general struggle to rewrite the past. The original composition, written by militants on the eve of independence, celebrated "the overthrow of colonialism," "the struggle against imperialism," and expressed confidence that "our country will be the graveyard of capitalism and exploitation." Its final stanza stressed that the labor "of workers and peasants will always produce wealth."[2] A 1983 revision had retained its celebration of socialism.[3]

The 1994 parliament, which included a number of RENAMO delegates, mandated a new national anthem that would reflect Mozambique's achievements without embodying any specific ideology. Chissano's administration launched a competition with a jury of both Frelimo and RENAMO representatives, the winner to receive a hefty prize of 25 million meticals. It took four years to reach an acceptable version, as writers and jury grappled with whether the text should break with the past or continue to celebrate past accomplishments. The final version referenced neither capitalist exploitation nor the struggles of workers and peasants, in favor of a nationalist message celebrating the people of Mozambique.[4]

Effacing Mozambique's socialist past necessarily meant diminishing the historical significance of Samora. After the newspaper accounts of Samora's death and long lines of people waiting for hours to pay their respects, after the moving photos of his burial and the family's grief, stories about the deceased president became increasingly rare. Coverage of Samora in *Tempo*, *Notícias*, and *Diário de Moçambique* dwindled. To be sure, his name was still invoked at Independence Day celebrations, there was some coverage on his birthday and the anniversary of his passing, and reporters periodically raised questions about his suspicious death.[5] Frelimo also organized nationwide events on the tenth, twentieth, and thirtieth anniversaries of the plane crash.[6] Samora had been reduced to an artifact of history. Looking back at Chissano's desire to establish his own identity free of "Samorismo," José Luís Cabaço, former minister of information, found this erasure inevitable: "The Chissano administration had to silence the past to guarantee the successful implementation of its new neoliberal policies."[7]

Twenty years after Samora's death and two years after Armando Guebuza came to power, Samora's image was resurrected and he was again honored in official circles. Ironically, this was part of a cynical ploy by Samora's former rival to increase his own popularity and reinforce his legitimacy as a nationalist leader. He linked himself and his administration to Samora in emphasizing their shared nationalist commitment, but at the same time ignored Samora's socialist policies.

Guebuza's maneuvers to exploit Samora's stature as the father of the country came in rapid succession. He ordered that Samora's face be placed on all new Mozambican currency and that monuments of him be built in every province as symbols of a resurgent Mozambican nationalism. In 2008 he orchestrated a national celebration of Samora's seventy-fifth birthday. Samora's image began to appear again on Frelimo posters and in Frelimo publications. Guebuza helped to establish the Samora Machel Documentation Center. Pro-government newspapers published retrospectives celebrating the deceased president, and his exploits figured prominently in the spate of memoirs written by both Samora's allies and ordinary citizens.[8]

Remembering from Below

Despite efforts to obliterate Samora's memory, it never truly died. In the decades after his death, his leadership was heralded in memoirs written by those who had fought alongside him. The Association of Ex-Combatants collected and archived oral accounts from its members of the armed struggle under Samora's leadership.

For their part, trade unionists were unprepared to have eviscerated all they had achieved during the socialist moment. They lamented the new pro-market policies that intensified economic hardship for their members as well as the short shrift given by Chissano's government to May Day celebrations, which Samora had made one of the cornerstones of popular culture. A 1997 letter to the editor published in *Notícias* under the title "Once upon a Time It Was the First of May" captured this sentiment. The writer said of May Day that "those were golden moments, and it is with great nostalgia that many workers like me remember those moments. There were parades all over the country, and especially in Maputo, where the demonstrations were of great importance."[9]

Samora and other fallen comrades were also remembered through public art. In 1996 a team of

Mozambicans led by architect José Forjaz constructed a memorial at Mbuzini to Samora and the thirty-four other Mozambicans who died with him. Spare in design, the thirty-five rusted steel poles rising from the crash site mark the brutality of the event, the suffering of family and friends, and the trauma of lost social and political accomplishments.[10]

Remembering from below was not limited to those who knew Samora personally or who had benefited from his socialist commitments. Nor was it felt only in southern Mozambique, where he was born and held in particularly high regard, but throughout the country. Many peasants and workers celebrated Samora's commitment to a just society—even as RENAMO supporters, sympathizers, and some Mozambican intellectuals railed against his harsh rule and failed socialist policies.[11]

During a visit to Mozambique in 2019, we encountered men and women wearing T-shirts, caps, headdresses, and loincloths emblazoned with Samora's portrait. "*Samora Vive*" (Samora Lives) was stamped on much of this apparel. Graffiti and drawings of the late president are common sights, and his image is preserved at historic sites. The most famous is in the panorama of Mozambican history located near the memorial in Maputo to Mozambique's fallen heroes. At the center of this massive mural are the faces of Samora and Eduardo Mondlane. Thousands pass it daily on their way to work or the airport.

Samora has also been memorialized through song, dance, theater, poetry, and pirated recordings of his speeches. Nowhere is the invocation of his name more prominent than in contemporary Mozambican rap music, particularly in Maputo.[12] Rap might seem an unlikely genre in which to salute Samora's legacy, since throughout the time he governed rap music was considered bourgeois decadence. His administration closed nightclubs where rap was performed, criticized artists who did not use revolutionary themes, attacked long hair and hip clothing, and associated rap with prostitution and drugs. Nevertheless, for many musicians Samora, in death, became a culture hero. In the late 1990s a new generation of artists disillusioned with postrevolutionary Mozambique began to lament Samora's passing and reminisce about his socialist ideology. "Samora Machel" by Xitiku ni Mbawula captures this sentiment.

> I hold a piece of paper to write freestyle
> I am invoking the great name of Samora Moíses Machel
> You died and left us freedom
> You died and left us with what you did
> You died fighting to eradicate the suffering of your
>   people
> Your name stays in my heart
> Everywhere I go your words keep me alive
> During your time children were like roses which would
>   never fade away
> but today it has all changed
> The roses now just fade away for lack of water.[13]

Mozambique's most popular artist, Azagaia, goes even further. In his video "Combatentes da fortuna" (Soldiers of fortune), in which he intersperses Samora's voice and image with his own singing, the fallen leader can be heard asking those accused of collaborating with the Portuguese to confess their errors. Paraphrasing

Samora's 1982 exhortation against corruption, the video lacerates the Guebuza administration: "It is impossible to develop welfare and happiness among thieves / they have to be chased away / and nobody chases them away except you [the people]."[14] As the video concludes, Azagaia passes in front of the image of Samora, marking his identification with the fallen leader. In live performances, Azagaia often dresses in military garb similar to Samora's to remind his audience of their ideological connections.

In our interview, Azagaia did acknowledge that Samora could be harsh and act like a dictator. When we asked him why Samora has become so popular among Mozambique's youth, he responded that Samora's legacy lives on because "he is a reference point, a symbol of the Mozambican nation; so we can be poor but still have our pride."[15] According to musicologist Janne Rantala, Samora's "speeches now belong to public memory and often return to the streets through voice recordings. He has been given a new political afterlife as a voice of criticism against current politics."[16]

Samora's speeches and singing are readily available on inexpensive pirated discs and cassettes. His speeches are often played on buses as a form of entertainment. Even in Beira, a RENAMO stronghold, two decades after his death six hundred people crowded into the São Jorge Theater for a film and discussion about Samora's life.[17]

A story shared by a former government minister captures the power of Samora's voice. Before the second swearing-in of President Chissano in 2002, technicians were testing the loudspeakers at Independence Square. To their surprise, the disc they were using contained one of Samora's speeches. When his voice was heard across much of downtown Maputo, throngs of Mozambicans rushed to the square in disbelief.[18]

In the countryside, traditional songs and poetry celebrate Samora, not only praising his bravery and commitment to the poor but offering commentary on contemporary Mozambican society. Years after his death, market women in southern Mozambique still sing about their profound sense of despair and sorrow.

Leader: Look at Botha
Chorus: Ya ya, yayayee
Leader: Look at Botha of South Africa.
Chorus: Ya oyoa, yaoyaoyee

Leader: He killed our President
Chorus: Ya, yayayee
Leader: Samora Moises Machel
Chorus: Ya ya, ya, ya, yee
Leader: Wi, wi, wiwee
Chorus: Wi, wi, wiwee

Leader: Botha, Botha, you have destroyed Mozam-
          bique, you have killed the great hero
          We are this day mourning this hero
          Our development has suffered a big setback
          Mozambique is full of ninjas [criminals]
          When Samora was alive there were no ninjas
          in this country
          Machel, we mourn you!
          We want you to enter our hearts so that your
          [teachings] will continue to bear fruit in
          the country
          The country has now turned upside down, as
          it has no owner [ruler]

Chorus: Look at Botha
          Yo, yo, yoyoyo!
          Look at Botha in South Africa
          Yo, yo, yoyoyo!

Leader:	Who sabotaged our aeroplane?
Chorus:	Yo, yo, yoyo!
Leader:	Look at Botha
Chorus:	Yo, yo, yoyoyo!
Leader:	He killed our hero
Chorus:	Yo, yo, yoyoyo![19]

More than a thousand miles away in Cabo Delgado, rural residents continue to mark Samora's passing with a similar refrain, stressing that his death was part of a long line of sacrifices that Frelimo leaders made so the country would be free.

Kulila wetu kulila Moshambiki
> *We cry, in Mozambique we cry*
Elo tunkulila kwetu
> *Yes, we cry*
Samora pakupela tutenda dashi
> *When Samora died, how could we do?*
Wetu vanang'olo tutenda dashi?
> *Us elders, how should we do?*

Wetu tundishanga shilambo shetu
> *We are desperate in our country,*
sha-Moshambiki
> *Mozambique*
Mwanashiva amalilike
> *Orphanhood must end*
Atunduvenge baba Mondlane kupela
> *Papa Mondlane died first*
Josina kupela
> *Then Josina died*
Tundishanga tunama dashi?
> *We are desperate, how to live?*

Akapele baba Mondlane
> *When papa Mondlane died*
Wapela mama Josina
> *And mama Josina died*
Tundishukulu
> *We were grateful*

Tundipata junji Samora Machele
> *to get Samora Machel*

Andidiva pamwe Mondlane
> *He substituted for Mondlane*

Wetu tundishukuru
> *We were grateful*

Continua yashimadengo
> *We carried on with the work*

Nelo tunkumbukila mwamboli wetu
> *Today we remember our liberator*

Tunkumbukila Samora
> *We remember Samora*

Angola na Tanzania
> *In Angola and Tanzania*

Ku-Zimbabwe
> *And in Zimbabwe*[20]

Their songs also affirm their adoration of the late president. In 2005, Paolo Israel recorded this Makonde celebration of "papa Machel's" life.

Kwaendile
> *Where he went*

Kwaendile baba Machele kwaendile
> *Where papa Machel went, where he went*

Ata kukalepa dashi
> *Even if it's far, then what?*

Wetu mwanda
> *We go*

Tummwoda baba Machel kwaendile kula
> *We follow papa Machel there, where he went*

Ata pakadingadinga dashi
> *It may be tortuous, so what?*

Tundapaleta pele
> *We will slip in*

Tummwoda baba Machel kwaendile akó
> *We follow papa Machel, where he went*

Mukaigwa kwaendile kushu kwanungu akulepa
> *And if you hear: he went far, at God's place, that's far*

Tuvene tupaleta vila pele
  Us, we'll just slip in
Kwannungu akulepa
  God's place, that's far away.[21]

In 2004, *mapiko* performers beseeched President Chissano not to forget them, but to come and visit their communities as Samora had on so many occasions.

Baba Chissano kukunagwela vyakutumidya
  Papa Chissano, you like to dispatch envoys
Shaida umwene
  You should come yourself
Utulole mwatunamila
  To see how we live
Mujo Samora ashindaida awenawena mudialudeya
  *Your friend Samora used to come and
  roam the villages*
Atulole mwatunamila
  To see how we live

Kanji wako:
  But you:
"Wena Chipande wena
  "Go, Chipande, go
Wena Raimundo wena
  Go, Raimundo go
'Kavalole mwavanamila"
  Have a look at how they live"[22]

In the aftermath of Samora's death, South Africans and Zimbabweans also paid homage to the fallen leader's memory through songs and poetry. Zimbabwean writer Musaemura Zimunya expresses his grief at Samora's death and celebrates his continued significance.

See now how they cry on the streets and tears fill
    the country
while they drink from your head and toast to the
    god of blood

as your children weep for your land and our destiny
they exult with song and braai and tumult in this loss.

In this end that is no end you will whisper com-
    rade, today, and tomorrow and tomorrow still
    you will whisper
beyond
the silence of the tomb and the crash
till your voice fills stadia of this land and many lands
and leaders to come
will proclaim in many voices of hope and wrath
    that's louder
than even the storm that thunders ever louder.
A luta! A luta! A luta continua![23]

These sentiments persist today. In June 2018, Allen engaged in numerous conversations with taxi drivers, street vendors, shoe shiners, and market women. Some described Samora as harsh or bemoaned his attacks on the Christian churches. All, however, emphasized his concern for the poor, his attempts to end the abusive practices of the colonial past, the power of his personality, and his infectious laughter. Perhaps a taxi driver put it best: "Samora could be harsh, but he was not corrupt. He would not have permitted all the corruption that exists today. He cared for us."[24]

Social media provides a new platform for the discussion and reshaping of Samora's memory. Posts on Facebook and Instagram about present-day corruption in Mozambique often include Samora's 1982 admonition regarding Guebuza's early accumulation of wealth: "If a leader builds a house, the people must demand to know where he got the money." Samora's thoughts on social justice, the public good, immorality, and racism are also summoned up on social media as commentary on Mozambique's present ills.[25]

Most of these positive representations of Samora come from Maputo, which has always been a Frelimo stronghold. Additional research is necessary to determine the depth of his popularity in other parts of the country.[26] In Beira, some rappers have criticized Samora. The well-known Beira rapper Y-Not, in "Tempo que passou" (Times past), a critique of the popular Frelimo song "Não vamos esquecer" (We will never forget), chastised Samora for his authoritarian practices that perpetuated colonial abuses.[27]

Conclusion

Samora's Life Revisited

Samora was a tragically flawed hero who brought independence and hope to millions of Mozambicans. Through personal experience and the writings of Mao Zedong, Frantz Fanon, Kwame Nkrumah, and Amilcar Cabral, he came to believe that colonialism and capitalism were inextricably interconnected. In different ways, each of these authors presented a powerful critique of imperialism and the colonial order and offered a blueprint for attacking class injustices and the colonizing of the mind. Nevertheless, Samora's socialism was always rooted in Mozambican reality. For him, the Mozambican revolution faced its own specific challenges, making it inappropriate to simply mimic other socialist nations.

Samora left an indelible mark on the young nation as a charismatic leader inspiring loyalty and a spirit of sacrifice. He used state power and the bully pulpit to attack illiteracy, disease, exploitation of women, and other forms of oppression. He introduced anticorruption policies, reminding Frelimo's leaders and cadres that they would be held accountable if they used their positions to accumulate wealth or influence. He also championed Frelimo's nonracial ideology and encouraged residents of Portuguese and Asian descent to become citizens of the new Mozambique.

It is equally clear that Samora relied both on heavy-handed tactics and the power of his personality to carry out Frelimo's policies. When Frelimo's socialist project lost credibility and the armed forces were unable to contain RENAMO, his administration became increasingly authoritarian. Its use of force to expand the communal village system and cleanse the cities of the "socially marginal" are examples. The reintroduction of corporal punishment, including whipping, remains a significant blemish on his record. History will not and should not forget the murders of Simango, Nkavandame, and Simião. Samora's refusal to permanently remove Guebuza and others from leadership positions after they had committed serious abuses of power also tarnished his presidency and created problems that continue until today.

Samora's tendency to dismiss African religious beliefs as obscurantist revealed his misunderstanding of their significance in many Mozambican communities. His assumption that persuasion and scientific rationalism would easily undermine indigenous and Christian beliefs was naïve, as was his confidence that Frelimo could construct a new moral order.

In his quest for economic and social justice, Samora was often myopic, convinced Mozambique could jump over history. Despite the dearth of financial experts, agronomists, and technical personnel, he believed that a state-run command economy could transform Mozambique's underdeveloped and distorted economic system. However laudable his attempts to restructure the health and educational sectors, the same lack of resources impeded their successful implementation.

But, Samora was also a realist. When socialist planning failed to meet the needs of the Mozambican people, Samora, rather than admitting defeat, searched for alternatives. Mozambique's move toward a mixed economy, which Samora oversaw, flowed directly from these setbacks—as did the recalibration of its relations with the wider world.

Samora's foreign policy aimed to protect both Mozambican sovereignty and its nonaligned status. This was not always possible. Because most Western governments supported Portugal during the armed struggle, FRELIMO had no choice but to seek military assistance from the Soviet Union and its allies. When Samora realized his young nation had become excessively dependent on Moscow, he resisted Soviet entreaties for a naval base in Mozambique, refused to become embroiled in the Sino-Soviet split, deepened Mozambique's involvement in the Non-Aligned Movement, strengthened ties with the Nordic countries, and used the Lancaster House negotiations resulting in Zimbabwe's independence to improve relations with the West. Nevertheless, he was unsuccessful in convincing the NATO allies to end their support for the apartheid regime that was seriously threatening Mozambique's sovereignty.

Perhaps his most significant foreign policy blunder was the bellicose rhetoric directed at South Africa, which provided it an excuse to intensify its destabilization campaign. While Samora's goal of dismantling apartheid was courageous and principled, it was highly unrealistic, given the imbalance in military power. Samora also miscalculated Pretoria's long-term commitment to RENAMO and RENAMO's destructive capacity. Both he and Mozambique paid a heavy price.

Two years before Samora's death, he reaffirmed that he would never forget for whom he was fighting: "I remain a 'guerrilla,' a combatant for the interests of my country, and of my people."[1] Today, Mozambican intellectuals, activists, and politicians of all stripes continue to debate how Samora should be remembered. He also figures prominently in the conversations, gossip, debates, and popular culture of many ordinary citizens. Although the memories that Mozambicans hold of their deceased leader are neither fixed nor uniform, more than thirty years after his death many still share his vision of a just society.

It remains to be seen whether Samora's vision of a society based on social and economic equality will ever be realized.

Notes

Prologue: The Challenge of Representation

1. When villagers began to discuss these abuses or any other sensitive political matters, we always turned off our tape recorder. We feared that, if the tapes or their transcriptions were confiscated, the elders would suffer harsh retributions.

2. For a pioneering study on life in the subúrbios, see David Morton, *Age of Concrete: Housing and the Shape of Aspiration in the Capital of Mozambique* (Athens: Ohio University Press, 2019).

3. An *assimilado* (assimilated person) was one who, by virtue of having adopted Portuguese cultural norms, enjoyed full rights of citizenship under the law. The term *padrinho* refers to a godfather or personal patron.

4. Graça Machel, interview, Maputo, n.d., Centro de Documentação Samora Machel (CDSM), folder 58.

5. During this period, Allen, Roberta Washington, William Minter, and Prexy Nesbitt organized the Mozambique Support Network to coordinate these efforts.

6. This is very similar to what feminist scholars define as "intersubjective knowledge." We are indebted to Heidi Gengenbach for this observation (personal communication, August 8, 2019).

7. Edward Said, *Representations of the Intellectual* (New York: Pantheon, 1994), 32.

8. The FRELIMO archives are housed at the Arquivo Histórico de Moçambique.

9. Marc Augé, *Oblivion*, trans. Marjolijn de Jager (Minneapolis: University of Minnesota Press, 2004), 18, quoted in Olga Shevchenko and Oksana Sarkisova, "Remembering Life in the Soviet Union, One Family Photo at a Time," *New York Times*,

December 27, 2017, https://www.nytimes.com/2017/12/27/opinion-soviet-union-one-photos.html.

10. See Mary Jo Maynes, "U.S. Labor History in Recent Biography," *Radical History Review* 72 (1998): 183.

Chapter 1: Living Colonialism

1. Raul Honwana, *The Life History of Raul Honwana* (Boulder, CO: Lynne Reiner, 1988), 105.

2. Thomas Henriksen, *Revolution and Counterrevolution: Mozambique's War of Independence* (Westport, CT: Greenwood, 1983), 219.

3. Eric Allina, *Slavery by Any Other Name: African Life under Company Rule in Colonial Mozambique* (Charlottesville: University of Virginia Press, 2012), 25.

4. Ibid., 151.

5. Allen Isaacman, *The Tradition of Resistance in Mozambique: The Zambesi Valley, 1850–1921*, in collaboration with Barbara Isaacman (Berkeley: University of California Press, 1976), 157–58.

6. Because the international banking community had established a relatively low fixed price for gold bullion, in sharp contrast to its mounting free-market price, Lisbon was able to sell gold on the open market in South Africa at several times its bullion value for three decades—earning an additional windfall from this arrangement. The funds generated were a major source of income for Portugal.

7. Toward this end, Portugal developed the port of Lourenço Marques as a gateway to the Transvaal and other South African markets. The port at Beira served a similar function for landlocked Southern Rhodesia.

8. C. M. Braun, May 1, 1946, CDSM, folder 64.

9. See A. H. Oliveira Marques, *History of Portugal*, vol. 2 (New York: Columbia University Press, 1972); António Figueiredo, *Portugal: Fifty Years of Dictatorship* (Harmondsworth, UK: Penguin, 1975); Hugh Kay, *Salazar and Modern Portugal* (London: Eyre and Spottiswoode, 1970).

10. See Leroy Vail and Landeg White, *Capitalism and Colonialism in Mozambique: A Study of Quelimane District* (Minneapolis: University of Minnesota Press, 1981), 247. The Portuguese state had implemented neo-mercantile policies even before Salazar. In 1929, Lisbon canceled the charter of the Niassa Company and the following year abolished the *prazo* system, under which large estates were leased to colonists. Neither added much to the national economy. Five years later, state authorities nationalized the holdings of the Mozambique Company and shortly thereafter introduced the Circular of 1942, which envisioned a more systematic use of "African labor for the public good." Malyn Newitt, *A History of Mozambique* (Bloomington: Indiana University Press, 1995), 445–62; Vail and White, *Capitalism*, 296.

11. *O brado africano* (Lourenço Marques), February 27, 1931.

12. Olívia Machel, interview, Maputo, March 7, 2019; Julius Nyerere to Samora Machel, February 25, 1984, CDSM, folder 24.

13. Iain Christie, *Samora Machel: A Biography* (London: Zed Press, 1987), 5.

14. Samora Machel, interview, Pemba, October 15, 1984.

15. Gerhard Liesegang, "Samora Moisés Machel: The Formative Years (1933–1963)," in *Samora: Man of the People,* ed. António Sopa (Maputo: Maguezo Editores, 2001), 19–29.

16. Mandande Moisés Machel, interview, Chilembene, February 20, 1979.

17. Christie, *Samora Machel,* 3.

18. Samora Machel to Oliver Tambo, June 5, 1984, CDSM, folder 8.

19. José Luís Cabaço, interview, Maputo, June 11, 2018.

20. Aurélio Chambale, interview, n.d., CDSM, folder 58.

21. Aurélio Manave, interview, n.d., CDSM, folder 58.

22. Samito Machel, interview, Maputo, March 23, 2019.

23. Aurélio Manave, interview.

24. Summarized in Christie, *Samora Machel,* 3.

25. Aurélio Manave, interview.

26. Liesegang, "Samora Moisés Machel," 23.

27. Ibid.

28. Samora Machel to Oliver Tambo, June 5, 1984, CDSM, folder 8.

29. See Allen Isaacman, *Cotton Is the Mother of Poverty* (Portsmouth, NH: Heineman, 1996).

30. Herb Shore, "Mondlane, Machel and Mozambique: From Rebellion to Revolution," *Africa Today* 21, no. 1 (Winter 1974): 7.

31. Otto Roesch, "Migrant Labour and Forced Rice Production in Southern Mozambique: The Colonial Peasantry of the Lower Limpopo Valley," *Journal of Southern African Studies* 17, no. 2 (June 1991): 239–70.

32. Christie, *Samora Machel*, 7.

33. Aurélio Manave, interview.

34. A copy of his draft registration card can be found in CDSM, folder 31.

Chapter 2: The Early Political Education of Samora Machel

1. For the story of his life, see Eduardo Mondlane, *The Struggle for Mozambique* (London: Zed Press, 1983); Janet Rae Mondlane, ed., *O eco da tua voz: Cartas editadas de Eduardo Mondlane*, vol. 1 (Maputo: Imprensa Universitária UEM, 2007).

2. For important studies of the gendered division of labor in the urban centers of colonial Mozambique, see Kathleen Sheldon, *Pounders of Grain: A History of Women, Work, and Politics in Mozambique* (Portsmouth, NH: Heinemann, 2002); and Jeanne Marie Penvenne, *Women, Migration and the Cashew Economy in Southern Mozambique, 1945–1975* (Oxford: James Currey, 2015).

3. António Mondlane, interview, n.d., CDSM, folder 58.

4. Aurélio Manave, interview.

5. Ibid.

6. Ibid.; António Mondlane, interview.

7. Aurélio Manave, interview.

8. João Ferreira, interview, n.d., CDSM, folder 58.

9. Aurélio Manave, interview.

10. Christie, *Samora Machel*, 11.

11. Aurélio Manave, interview.

12. Ibid.

13. Derived from interviews with António Mondlane, Aurélio Manave, and João Ferreira; see also Matias Mboa, *Memórias da luta clandestina* (Maputo: Marimbique, 2009).

14. Liesegang, "Samora Moisés Machel," 13.

15. Graça Machel, interview.

16. For a detailed account of his experiences on Inhaca, see Ana Piedade Monteiro et al., *Samora Machel na ilha de Inhaca (1955—1959)* (Maputo: Imprensa Universitária UEM, 2012).

17. David Chainkomo, interview, n.d., CDSM, folder 58.

18. Ibid.; Olívia Machel, interview.

19. Barry Munslow, ed., *Samora Machel, an African Revolutionary: Selected Speeches and Writings* (London: Zed Press, 1995), xii.

20. Magarida Buque, interview, n.d., CDSM, folder 58.

21. Graça Machel, interview, Maputo, March 24, 2019.

22. This material is derived from Liesegang, "Samora Moisés Machel," 24—25.

23. António Alves Gomes, interview, Maputo, June 11, 2018.

24. Margarida Buque, interview.

25. Chissano was born in Chibuto in Gaza Province and attended high school at Liceu Salazar, where he became active in NESAM. He briefly studied medicine in Lisbon, where he met other anti-colonial nationalists from Angola and Guinea-Bissau. Under surveillance by the secret police, he fled to France and then joined FRELIMO. Joaquim Alberto Chissano, *Vidas, lugares e tempos* (Maputo: Texto Editores, 2010).

26. Guebuza was born in Nampula. His father was a nurse. At eight, his family moved to Lourenço Marques. He became president of NESAM in 1963 and on his second attempt successfully fled to Dar es Salaam via Swaziland, South Africa, Bechuanaland, and Zambia. When he arrived in Dar es Salaam he joined FRELIMO. Colin Darch, *Historical Dictionary of Mozambique* (Lanham, MD: Rowman and Littlefield, 2019), 180–81.

27. Magaia was born in Mocuba in Zambézia Province. His father was a nurse who moved around the country. While attending high school in Lourenço Marques, he joined NESAM

and became a leading militant within the organization. Darch, *Historical Dictionary*, 238–39.

28. Matsinhe was born in Casula in Tete Province where his father taught at a missionary school. In 1950, he moved to Lourenço Marques, attended high school there, and became actively involved in NESAM. Ibid., 400.

29. Born in Lourenço Marques, Honwana was active in NESAM and was a leading voice of cultural nationalism, as well as Mozambique's most prominent writer. In 1964, he published *Nós matámos o cão-tinhoso*, subsequently translated as *We Killed Mangy-Dog*. He was arrested in 1967 for subversive activities "in support of FRELIMO and against Portuguese sovereignty in Mozambique" and was imprisoned for several years. After his release, he went to Lisbon and subsequently fled to Tanzania, where he began his military training at Nachingwea. Raul Honwana, *The Life History of Raul Honwana* (Boulder, CO: Lynne Reiner, 1988), 165.

30. João Ferreira, interview.

31. Luís Bernardo Honwana, interview, Maputo, March 11, 1979; Esperança Abatar Muethemba, interview, April 15, 1979; Albino Magaia, interview, June 7, 1979. The latter two interviews were conducted by Isabel María Casimiro as part of a senior seminar on popular resistance Allen Isaacman taught at the Universidade Eduardo Mondlane.

32. Chissano, *Vidas, lugares e tempos*, 178.

33. Christie, *Samora Machel*, 13.

34. Of Portuguese descent, Ferreira served in the colonial army and then became a salesman for a pharmaceutical company. He befriended Samora when Samora worked as a nurse at Miguel Bombarda Hospital and warned Samora of his impending arrest by PIDE (João Ferreira, interview).

35. Veloso was born to a Portuguese family in Lourenço Marques. He went to Portugal in 1955 to train as an air force pilot and then returned to Mozambique. While in the Portuguese air force there, he hijacked a plane and flew it to Tanzania, where he joined FRELIMO. Jacinto Veloso, *Memories at Low Altitude* (Cape Town: Zebra Press, 2012).

36. Born in Lourenço Marques to an immigrant family from Goa, Nogar was a poet and early proponent of Mozambican cultural nationalism. Darch, *Historical Dictionary*, 294.

37. Born in Lourenço Marques, Cabaço attended law school in Lisbon and studied sociology in Italy, where in 1966 he made contact with FRELIMO. José Luís Cabaço, *Moçambique: Identidade, colonialismo e libertação* (São Paulo: Editora Unesp, 2009).

38. Born in the Mozambican capital, Balthazar was a highly respected lawyer who defended several prominent political prisoners. Darch, *Historical Dictionary*, 257.

39. Honorata Simão Tchussa, João Velemo Nunguanbe, and Jacob Jeremias Nyambir, interviews, Maputo, March 27, 2019.

40. Cornélio João Mandande, interview, Mueda, July 30, 1979; Zacarias Vanomoba, interview, Mueda, August 2, 1979; João Bonifácio, interview, Mueda, August 2, 1979.

41. Mondlane, *Struggle for Mozambique*, 118. Other estimates of the number of deaths ranged from seventeen to five hundred (Yussuf Adam and H. A. Dyutie, eds., "Entrevista: O massacre de Mueda: Falam testemunhas," *Arquivo: Boletim do Arquivo Histórico de Moçambique* 14 [October 1993]: 117–28). For an important reinterpretation of the events surrounding the Mueda massacre, see Paolo Israel, "The Matter of Return: The Mueda Massacre in Colonial Intelligence" (forthcoming).

42. Honorata Simão Tchussa, interview.

43. Cornélio João Mandande, interview.

44. Many of the older militants had lived abroad for more than a decade. Matthew Michinis and Mamole Lawrence Malinga initially led the militant group, which also enjoyed the support of the powerful Makonde chief Lazaro Nkavandame.

45. Paolo Israel, personal communication, August 12, 2019.

46. Lopes Tembe Ndelana, *From UDENAMO to FRELIMO and Mozambican Diplomacy* (Terra Alta, WV: Headline Books, 2016), *passim*; João Velemo Nunguanbe, interview.

47. Ndelana, *From UDENAMO*, 40.

48. Simango was the son of a Protestant minister who had been an outspoken critic of colonial abuses. Following in his father's footsteps, he was arrested in 1953 and three years later

was ordained in the Church of Christ. Simango rejected a scholarship to study in Lisbon because he thought it would deflect from his political agenda. Instead, he fled to Salisbury, Southern Rhodesia, joined UDENAMO, and reached out to Joshua Nkomo, leader of the Zimbabwe African Peoples Union, and Kwame Nkrumah, president of Ghana. Barnabé Lucas Ncomo, *Uria Simango: Um homem, uma causa* (Maputo: Edições Nováfrica, 2003).

49. Santos was born in 1929 in Lumbo, near the Island of Mozambique, to an Afro-Goan family. His father was an activist in the Associação Africana. He spent much of his youth in Lourenço Marques and in 1947 went to Portugal to study at the Instituto Superior Téchnico, where he met Africans and Asians from the Portuguese colonies who were members of the Casa dos Estudantes do Império. In 1951 Marcelino escaped to France. In Paris he played a pivotal role in the Federation of African Students, which was closely aligned with the French Communist Party. In 1955 he helped organize the Movimento Anti-Colonialista and in 1961 he was elected secretary-general of the Conference of Nationalist Organizations of the Portuguese Colonies, which superseded MAC. Based in Algeria, CONCP was an umbrella organization coordinating diplomatic and military support for the principal liberation movements seeking independence from Lisbon. Marcelino Dos Santos, interview, Maputo, March 2003.

50. See Helder Martins, *Porquê Sakrani? Memórias dum médico duma guerrilha esquecida* (Maputo: Editorial Terceiro Milénia, 2001).

51. Alberto Joaquim Chipande, interview, n.d., CDSM, folder 58.

52. FRELIMO, Dept. of Information, "Editorial: 25th of June, the Starting Point," *Mozambique Revolution*, no. 51 (June 1972): 1.

53. Liesegang, "Samora Moisés Machel," 25.

54. Mboa, *Memórias*, 85.

55. João Ferreira, interview.

56. Margarida Buque, interview.

57. This was true not only of young men but also of the small number of young women who fled. Among them was Josina Muthemba, whom Samora married in 1969.

58. Olívia Machel, interview.

59. Graça Machel, interview.

60. Mboa, *Memórias*, 86–87.

61. Christie, *Samora Machel*, 23.

Chapter 3: The Struggle within the Struggle, 1962–70

1. FRELIMO, Dept. of Information, "Editorial: 25th of June, the Starting Point," *Mozambique Revolution*, no. 51 (June 1972): 1.

2. Raimundo Pachinuapa, interview, n.d., CDSM, folder 58.

3. Mboa, *Memórias*, 87–88.

4. Alberto Joaquim Chipande, interview.

5. Jacob Jeremias Nyambir, interview, Maputo, March 27, 2019.

6. José Manuel Duarte de Jesus, *Eduardo Mondlane: Hope Destroyed* (self-pub., CreateSpace, 2016), 291.

7. Raimundo Pachinuapa, interview.

8. Jacob Jeremias Nyambir, interview.

9. Ibid.

10. Ibid.

11. Ibid.

12. Raimundo Pachinuapa, interview; Jacob Jeremias Nyambir, interview.

13. Alberto Chipande, interview.

14. Jacob Jeremias Nyambir, interview.

15. This group, representing a majority of the FRELIMO leadership, included Marcelino dos Santos, Joaquim Chissano, Armando Guebuza, and the senior military commanders Filipe Samuel Magaia, Alberto Chipande, Raimundo Pachinuapa, Jorge Rebelo, and Samora.

16. Oscar Monteiro, interview, Matola, March 26, 2019; Duarte de Jesus, *Eduardo Mondlane*, 24–26, 636–37.

17. For a detailed discussion of the opposition within FRELIMO, drawing on reports from Portuguese, Soviet Union,

Chinese, and East German intelligence operatives based in Tanzania, see Duarte de Jesus, *Eduardo Mondlane*, 263–344.

18. Born in 1904, Nkavandame founded the Liguilanilu cooperative. He contacted MANU soon after its formation and later fled to Tanzania with many of his followers. In June 1963 he was appointed to the FRELIMO Central Committee with a mandate to promote trade in the liberated zones and between the liberated zones and Tanzania. Darch, *Historical Dictionary*, 292.

19. Edward Alpers, "Islam in the Service of Colonialism? Portuguese Strategy during the Armed Liberation Struggle in Mozambique," *Lusotopie*, no. 6 (1999): 165–84.

20. Duarte de Jesus, *Eduardo Mondlane*, 270–77.

21. Alberto Chipande, interview.

22. Helder Martins returned to Tanzania to work as a FRELIMO doctor. Martins, *Porquê Sakrani?*, 265–99.

23. Fernandes's racial hatred may have been the reason for his later expulsion from FRELIMO. Thomas Henriksen, *Revolution and Counterrevolution: Mozambique's War of Independence* (Westport, CT: Greenwood, 1983), 24–25. Although Chai is considered the beginning of the armed struggle in FRELIMO lore, Paolo Israel, a researcher working in northern Mozambique, has collected evidence indicating that MANU guerrillas had attacked a Portuguese location inside Mozambique in 1960 (personal communication, August 13, 2019).

24. Barbara Cornwell, *The Bush Rebels* (London: André Deutsch, 1973), 53–54.

25. Jacob Jeremias Nyambir, interview.

26. For a history of the Mozambican Institute and the racial, cultural, and linguistic divisions within it, see Felipe B. C. C. Bastos, "Políticas de língua e movimentos nacionalistas: Campos de interação histórica entre Tanzânia e Moçambique (1961–1969)" (master's thesis, Universidade Estadual de Campinas, 2018), 191–241.

27. William Minter, "Report on meeting with Forms l and Forms ll, an analysis of reasons for discontent among the students" (unpublished document in authors' possession, January 19, 1968).

28. Douglas L. Wheeler, "A Document for the History of African Nationalism: The UNEMO 'White Paper' of 1968, a

Student Reply to Eduardo Mondlane's 1967 Paper," *African Historical Studies* 3, no. 1 (1970): 169–80.

29. Hama Thay, interview, Maputo, June 20, 2018.

30. Field Notebook of Samora Machel, 1965–67, CDSM, folder 66.

31. Simango's biographer, Barnabé Lucas Ncomo, describes the contempt in which Samora's opponents held him. Ncomo, *Uria Simango*, 141–42.

32. Samora Machel, interview, Maputo, May 7, 1979.

33. Christie, *Samora Machel*, 123.

34. José Luís Cabaço, interview, Maputo, June 13, 2018.

35. According to Jacob Jeremias Nyambir, who was walking in front of Magaia in a dry riverbed when shots rang out, Magaia thought he had been wounded by a grenade. Efforts to revive him failed. When the platoon's weapons were examined, a guerrilla whose gun barrel was still hot and smelled of gunpowder was arrested (Jacob Jeremias Nyambir, interview). Lourenço Matola spent five years in prison before escaping and fleeing to Kenya. The findings of a FRELIMO inquiry into the murder have never been made public, leading to an array of rumors about who was responsible for his death (personal communication, Paolo Israel, August 12, 2019).

36. Oscar Monteiro, interview, Matola, March 6, 2019.

37. Christie, *Samora Machel*, 57.

38. For an analysis of events surrounding Mondlane's murder, see George Roberts, "The Assassination of Eduardo Mondlane: FRELIMO, Tanzania, and the Politics of Exile in Dar es Salaam," *Cold War Histories* 17 (2017): 1–19.

39. Ncomo, *Uria Simango*, 400.

40. According to Ncomo, Simango's downfall can be traced to the greed for power of the south-regionalist wing, allied with the Goan, *mestiço*, and white Marxists. Ibid.

41. Ibid., 193–97.

Chapter 4: Samora and the Armed Struggle, 1964–75

1. Raimundo Pachinuapa, interview.

2. Ibid.; Alberto Joaquim Chipande, interview.

3. Darch, *Historical Dictionary*, 283.

4. Helder Martins, "Samora na Luta Armada (1965–68)," in António Sopa, *Samora: Homen do Povo*, 111.

5. Oscar Monteiro, interview, March 6, 2019.

6. Field Notebook of Samora Machel, 1965–67, CDSM, folder 66.

7. For a discussion of these issues, see CDSM, folder 1.

8. See Samora Machel, "Nota de estudos para os instructores: Comprender a nossa tarefa," December 6, 1970, CDSM, folder 2: Documentos a FRELIMO; and Aquino de Bragança and Immanuel Wallerstein, *Quem é o inimigo?* (Lisbon: Iniciativas Editoriais, 1978), 201–25.

9. Interview with anonymous insubordinate student, n.d., collected by Paolo Israel.

10. Samora Machel to Josina Machel, October 22, 1970, CDSM, folder 4.

11. Christie, *Samora Machel*, 38–41; Sayaka Funada-Classen, *The Origins of War in Mozambique: A History of Unity and Division* (Oxford: African Minds, 2013), 298–301.

12. See Isaacman, *Tradition of Resistance*, 199.

13. Field Notebook of Samora Machel.

14. Martins, *Porque Sakani?*, 265–98.

15. FRELIMO, Dept. of Information, "Shaping the Political Line," *Mozambique Revolution*, no. 51 (June 1972): 18.

16. Cornwell, *Bush Rebels*, 93.

17. Ibid., 65.

18. Funada-Classen, *Origins of War in Mozambique*, 319.

19. Henriksen, *Revolution and Counterrevolution*, 118.

20. See *Biografia oficial de Josina Machel*, n.d., CDSM, folder 31; and Renato Matussa and Josina Malique, *Josina Machel* (Maputo: ARPAC, 2007).

21. Samora Machel to Josina Machel, October 22, 1970, CDSM, folder 4.

22. "Resolucões sobre ritos de iniciação," Segunda Conferência de Departmento da Defesa, February 20, 1971, CDSM, folder 2.

23. Samora Machel, *Mozambique: Sowing the Seeds of Revolution* (London: Committee for Freedom in Mozambique,

Angola and Guiné, 1975), 24; emphasis in original. For a history of the Organização da Mulher Moçambicana, see Helena Hansen, Ragnar Hansen, Ole Gjerstad, and Chantal Sarazin, "The Organization of Mozambican Women," *Journal of Eastern African Research and Development* 15 (1985): 230–44.

24. Civilians were inadvertently killed by land mines, which were one of the most effective tactical tools at the guerrillas' disposal (Alberto Chipande, interview).

25. Manuel Braz da Costa, interview, Lichinga, August 15, 1980.

26. Ibid.; Henriksen, *Revolution and Counterrevolution*, 123. Henriksen notes that when FRELIMO forces entered the settler zones of Manica and Sofala, they killed a white settler and his wife and there were also some attacks on European farms. While FRELIMO leaders publicly denied them, they privately acknowledged the attacks, claiming they were mistakes (127).

27. Allen Isaacman and Barbara Isaacman, *Dams, Displacement and the Delusion of Development* (Athens: Ohio University Press, 2013), 89.

28. Funada-Classen, *Origins of War in Mozambique*, 319.

29. Mondlane, *The Struggle for Mozambique*, 178.

30. Maria Teresa Veloso, interview, Maputo, August 24, 1977.

31. Samora Machel, interview, May 7, 1979.

32. Interview with Helder Martins, *World Medicine* 12 (January 26, 1977): 22.

33. FRELIMO, Dept. of Information, "Shaping the Political Line," *Mozambique Revolution*, no. 51 (June 1972): 25.

34. On the devastating effects of the forced cotton regime, see Allen Isaacman, *Cotton Is the Mother of Poverty* (Portsmouth, NH: Heinemann, 1996).

35. Samora Machel, *Mozambique: Sowing the Seeds*, 72–73.

36. Funada-Classen, *Origins of War in Mozambique*, 326–27.

37. The only exceptions were those few aldeamentos that were turned into model villages for propaganda purposes.

38. João Paulo Borges Coelho, "Protected Villages and Communal Villages in the Mozambican Province of Tete (1968–1982): A History of State Resettlement Policies, Development and War" (PhD thesis, University of Bradford, 1993), 160–69.

39. Ibid., 205. See also Arquivo Histórico de Moçambique, FMA, Cx. 107, Secretário Provincial de Terras e Povoamento, "Criação de um grupo de trabalho coordenador dos aldeamentos," December 22, 1971.

40. Peter Size and Fedi Alfante, joint interview, Chinyanda Nova, May 25, 1998.

41. *Australian*, no. 2359, February 3, 1972, in Arquivo Nacional de Torre do Tombo (ANTT), PIDE/DGSSC, Proc. 8743, CI (2), folder 2.

42. W. Nusey, "The War in Tete: A Threat to All in Southern Africa," *Johannesburg Star*, July 1, 1972.

43. Mustafa Dhada, *The Portuguese Massacre of Wiriyamu in Colonial Mozambique, 1964–2013* (New York: Bloomsbury Academic, 2016).

44. The Portuguese also paid a price, with over 130 soldiers killed and double that number seriously wounded.

45. Alberto Chipande, interview, CDSM.

46. Samora Machel to Josina Machel, October 20, 1970, CDSM, folder 4.

47. Barry Munslow, ed., *Samora Machel, an African Revolutionary: Selected Speeches and Writings* (London: Zed Press, 1995), xvii.

48. Samito Machel, interview, Maputo, March 25, 2019.

49. Ibid.

50. Oscar Monteiro, interview, March 26, 2019.

51. Ibid.

52. Christie, *Samora Machel*, 82.

53. Ibid., 83.

54. Ibid., 84.

55. FRELIMO was represented by Oscar Monteiro, the only lawyer involved in the armed struggle. The Portuguese delegation included Melo Atunes from the Armed Forces Movement and Almeida dos Santos, a member of the anti-Salazar opposition now minister of overseas coordination.

56. Oscar Monteiro, interview, March 26, 2019.

57. Isaacman and Isaacman, *Dams, Displacement*, 150–87.

58. A decade later, he articulated his concerns more fully in Aquino de Bragança, "Independência sem descolonização: A

transferência do poder em Moçambique, notas sobre os seus antecedentes" (paper presented at the conference "African Independence: Origins and Consequences of the Transfer of Power, 1956–1980," University of Zimbabwe, Harare, January 1985).

59. Henriksen, *Revolution and Counterrevolution*.

60. Munslow, *Samora Machel*, 5.

61. Ibid., 3.

62. Colin Darch and David Hedges, "Political Rhetoric in the Transition to Mozambican Independence: Samora Machel in Beira, June 1975," *Kronos* 39, no. 1 (2013): 41.

63. Ibid., 57.

64. Honwana, *Life History*, 171.

65. Paul Fauvet and Marcelo Mosse, *Carlos Cardoso: Telling the Truth in Mozambique* (Cape Town: Double Storey, 2003), 24.

66. Olívia Machel, interview, March 7, 2019.

Chapter 5: Politics, Performance, and People's Power, 1975–ca. 1977

1. Olívia Machel, interview, March 7, 2019.

2. Benedict Anderson, *Imagined Communities: Reflections on the Origin and Spread of Nationalism* (London: Verso, 1988).

3. *Review of African Political Economy* 2 (1975): 3.

4. António Alves Gomes, interview, Maputo, June 13, 2018.

5. Graça Simbine was born in Gaza in 1945. She went to a missionary school for primary education and was the only African in her class in Liceu António Enes, her high school, gaining the highest score in Mozambique in the national French examination. She studied at the Universidade de Lisboa and joined FRELIMO in 1973. Two years later, at the age of thirty, she became Mozambique's first minister of education and culture. She married Samora later that year. Graça Machel, interview.

6. Samora Machel, *The Tasks Ahead: Selected Speeches of Samora Machel* (New York: Afro American Information Service, 1975), 4.

7. This term is derived from Kelly Askew, *Performing the Nation: Swahili Music and Cultural Politics in Tanzania* (Chicago: University of Chicago Press, 2002).

8. Luís Bernardo Honwana, interview, Maputo, March 7, 2019.

9. Christie, *Samora Machel*, 170.

10. Malyn Newitt, *A Short History of Mozambique* (London: Oxford University Press, 2017), 156.

11. Rui Assubuji, "Samora's Legacy in Kok Nam's Photography" (paper presented at the conference "The Living Legacies of Samora Machel," Centre for Humanities Research, University of Western Cape, February 12, 2019).

12. Quoted in Paul Fauvet and Marcelo Mosse, *Carlos Cardoso: Telling the Truth in Mozambique* (Cape Town: Double Storey, 2003), 50.

13. António Pinto de Abreu, *Algumas das memórias que eu ainda retenho* (Maputo: Madeira e Madeira, 2017), 76.

14. Sarah Lefanu, *S Is for Samora: A Lexical Biography of Samora Machel and the Mozambican Dream* (New York: Columbia University Press, 2012), 107–8.

15. Rui Assubuji and Patricia Hayes, "The Political Sublime: Reading Kok Nam, Mozambican Photographer (1939–2012)," *Kronos* 39, no. 1 (2013): 66–111. This performance was not unique to Samora. Leaders on the left and right from Castro to Mussolini have been depicted tilling the land and engaged in other critical labor for the nation.

16. Samora Machel, "A Nossa Luta," *Notícias de Beira*, June 7, 1975.

17. Oscar Monteiro, the senior legal advisor in the Lusaka Accord negotiations, was only thirty-three. Prakash Ratilal was four years younger when he was appointed the principal monetary official and vice governor of the Central Bank. Oscar Monteiro, interview, Matola, March 21, 2019; Prakash Ratilal, interview, Maputo, March 16, 2019.

18. Samora Machel, *Establishing People's Power to Serve the Masses* (Dar es Salaam: Tanzania Publishing House, 1977), 7.

19. Roberta Washington, personal communication, New York, August 26, 2019.

20. Benedito Luís Machava, "The Morality of Revolution: Urban Cleanup Campaigns, Reeducation Camps, and Citizenship in Socialist Mozambique (1974–1988)" (PhD diss., University of Michigan, 2018), 202.

21. On how colonial and postcolonial states defined "wicked women," see Dorothy L. Hodgson and Sheryl A. McCurdy, *"Wicked" Women and the Reconfiguration of Gender in Africa* (Portsmouth, NH: Heinemann, 2001).

22. Machava, "Morality of Revolution," 18.

23. Ibid., 15.

24. *Tempo* (Maputo), January 1, 1978, 53–54.

25. Michael T. Kaufman, "Mozambique Is Viewed as Africa's Best Hope for the Flowering of Socialism's 'New Man,'" *New York Times*, November 14, 1977.

26. Fernando Ganhão, "Samora," in *Samora: Man of the People,* ed. António Sopa (Maputo: Maguezo Editores, 2001), 17.

27. Helder Martins, *Porquê Sakrani? Memórias dum médico duma guerrilha esquecida* (Maputo: Editorial Terceiro Milénia, 2001), 91.

28. Darch, *Historical Dictionary*, 80.

29. Teodato Hunguana, interview, Maputo, June 21, 2018.

30. João Ferreira, interview.

31. Samora also engaged in serious private discussions with Cardoso. For an excellent study of his life and career, see Fauvet and Mosse, *Carlos Cardoso*. According to Graça Machel, "they had a strong intellectual relationship—even when they disagreed" (63).

32. In 1981, the government established a commission to impose guidelines limiting who had access to the stores, how much each family could purchase, and what products would be available.

33. José Luís Cabaço, interview.

34. Ibid.

35. Samora Machel, "Knowledge and Science Should Be for the Total Liberation of Man," *Race & Class* 19, no. 4 (1978): 400.

36. Samora Machel, *Fazer de escola uma base para o povo tomar o poder* (Maputo: Instituto Naçional dos Livros e Discos, 1979), 11–12.

37. Samora Machel, interview, May 7, 1979.

38. Judith Marshall, *Literacy, Power, and Democracy in Mozambique: The Governance of Learning from Colonization to the Present* (Boulder, CO: Westview, 1993), 91–103.

39. Judite Frederico de Almeida e Faria to Samora Machel, June 25, 1975, CDSM, folder 17.

40. José Luís Cabaço, "The New Man," in Sopa, *Samora: Man of the People*, 106.

41. Ibid., 103–11.

42. "Song for Samora," n.d., CDSM, folder 29.

43. Samora Machel, "Knowledge and Science," 400.

44. UNICEF/WHO Joint Committee on Health Policy, *National Decision-Making for Primary Health Care* (Geneva: WHO, 1981).

45. Alexandre Gonçalves, "Priorité à la médecine préventive," *Afrique-Asie* 217 (July 1980): 47.

46. David Morton, *Age of Concrete: Housing and the Shape of Aspiration in the Capital of Mozambique* (Athens: Ohio University Press, 2019), 220.

47. Allen Isaacman and Barbara Isaacman, *Mozambique: From Colonialism to Revolution* (Boulder, CO: Westview, 1983), 139.

48. Similar problems plagued the literacy campaign. As one Canadian teacher noted, "the path proved to be both jagged and uneven, marked by advances and retreats and holds." (Marshall, *Literacy, Power, and Democracy*, 267).

49. By 1975, Mozambique was importing twice what it exported, the trade deficit had ballooned to $50 million, and the gross national product had dropped by 17 percent. Jens Erik Torp, *Industrial Planning and Development in Mozambique* (Uppsala: Scandinavian Institute of African Studies, 1979), 31.

50. Prakash Ratilal, "O processo de adesão de Moçambique às instituições de Bretton Woods" (unpublished paper, Maputo, April 30, 2010), 5.

51. See Isabel Casimiro, *"Paz na terra, guerra em casa": Feminismo e organizaçãoes de mulheres em Moçambique* (Recife: Editora UFPE, 2014).

52. Graça Machel, interview, March 24, 2019.

53. Ibid.

54. Ibid.

55. Olívia, Jucelina, and Ornila Machel, joint interview, Maputo, March 15, 2019; Samito Machel, interview, Maputo, March 23, 2019.

56. Olívia, Jucelina, and Ornila Machel, joint interview.

57. Olívia Machel, interview, March 7, 2019.

58. Samora Machel, interview, May 7, 1979.

59. Olívia Machel, interview, Maputo, March 8, 2019. Jucelina, an outstanding runner, represented Mozambique in the 1980 Olympics. Edelson was considered one of the country's best swimmers.

60. Graça Machel, interview, March 24, 2019.

61. Nyeleti to Graça and Samora, September 23, 1981, CDSM, folder 8.

62. Hama Thay, interview.

63. Teodato Hunguana, interview.

Chapter 6: Samora Machel's Marxism and the Defense of the Revolution, 1977–82

1. Samora Machel, "The People's Democratic Revolutionary Process," in *Samora Machel, an African Revolutionary: Selected Speeches and Writings*, ed. Barry Munslow (London: Zed Press, 1995), 42.

2. Sílvia Bragança, *Aquino de Bragança: Batalhas ganhas, sonhos a continuar* (Maputo: Ndjira, 2009), 277–78.

3. See Julius Nyerere, *Freedom and Unity: Uhuru na Umoja* (Oxford: Oxford University Press, 1966).

4. In a conversation with Allen Isaacman and Iain Christie, Samora insisted that "the main characteristic of a socialist society is the establishment of cooperation and fraternity among men." Samora Machel, interview, May 7, 1979.

5. José Luis Cabaço, interview, June 11, 2018.

6. Oscar Monteiro, interview, March 5, 2019. See also Jorge Rebelo to Graça Machel, n.d., Centro de Documentação Samora Machel (CDSM), folder 27.

7. After Samora's death, Chissano and Guebuza dropped any pretense of being Marxists. Both returned to the church and became wealthy property owners, as did many of their former comrades.

8. Agência de Informação de Moçambique, *Information Bulletin* 9–10 (1977): 6.

9. Ibid., 11.

10. Samora Machel, interview, May 7, 1979.

11. Frelimo, *Central Committee Report to the Third Congress of Frelimo* (London: Mozambique, Angola, Guinea-Bissau Information Centre, 1978), 43–44.

12. Samora Machel, interview, May 7, 1979.

13. Frelimo, *Central Committee Report*, 216.

14. *Notícias* (Maputo), August 28, 1982.

15. Otto Roesch, "Socialism and Rural Development in Mozambique: The Case of Aldeia Communal 24 de Julho" (PhD diss., University of Toronto, 1986), *passim*.

16. M. Anne Pitcher, *Transforming Mozambique: The Politics of Privatization, 1975–2000* (Cambridge: Cambridge University Press, 2002), 95.

17. Alice Dinerman, *Revolution, Counter-revolution and Revisionism in Post-colonial Africa: The Case of Mozambique, 1975–1994* (London: Routledge, 2015), 68.

18. Paul Fauvet, personal communication, Maputo, July 13, 2019.

19. *Notícias* (Maputo), August 20, 1982.

20. In Gaza's Communal Village Eduardo Mondlane, 35 percent of the cooperative members worked collectively fifty days or less in a year (*Notícias* [Maputo], June 25, 1982).

21. David Ottaway and Marina Ottaway, *Afrocommunism* (New York: Africana, 1981), 87.

22. Samora Machel, interview, May 7, 1979.

23. Merle L. Bowen, "Peasant Agriculture in Mozambique: The Case of Chokwe, Gaza Province," *Canadian Journal of African Studies* 23, no. 3 (1989): 355–79.

24. Marcia Catherine Schenck, "Socialist Solidarities and Their Afterlives: Histories and Memories of Angolan and Mozambican Migrants in the German Democratic Republic, 1975–2015" (PhD diss., Princeton University, 2019), 44.

25. These ideas were stressed in a speech by Graça Machel, minister of education, to students leaving for Cuba in 1977 (*Notícias* [Maputo], September 3, 1977).

26. Ratilal, "O processo de adesão," 7.

27. Business International, *Mozambique: On the Road to Reconstruction and Development* (Geneva: Business International, 1980), 50–51.

28. Pitcher, *Transforming Mozambique*, 82.

29. Joseph Hanlon, *Mozambique: Who Calls the Shots?* (Bloomington: Indiana University Press, 1991), 12.

30. Ratilal, "O processo de adesão," 5.

31. Hanlon, *Mozambique*, 7–11.

32. Prakash Ratilal, interview, Maputo, March 23, 2019. These talks broke down when Samora rejected demands that Mozambique end food subsidies and reduce expenditures on health, education, and housing. The parties did reach agreement in 1985.

33. Samora Machel, interview, May 7, 1979.

34. Samora Machel, *Establishing People's Power to Serve the Masses* (Dar es Salaam: Tanzania Publishing House, 1977), 7.

35. Samora Machel, interview, May 7, 1979.

36. Samora Machel, "Make Beira the Starting-Point for an Organizational Offensive," in Munslow, *Samora Machel*, 73.

37. António Alves Gomes, interview, Maputo, March 3, 2019.

38. Included among the "compromised" were a small number of FRELIMO supporters who had been imprisoned by the Portuguese. Because they had not participated in political education during the armed struggle, some were initially considered suspect. See Benedito Luís Machava, "State Discourse on Internal Security and the Politics of Punishment in Post-Independence Mozambique (1975–1983)," *Journal of Southern African Studies* 37, no. 3 (2011): 60.

39. António Alves Gomes, interview, March 3, 2019.

40. "Para compreender as crimas contra o povo e do estado," *Tempo* (Maputo), March 18, 1979, 18–22.

41. Frelimo, *Central Committee Report*, supp. 6.

42. Samora Machel, speech at the Sixth Conference of Heads of State and Government of the Non-Aligned Countries, Havana, Cuba, September 4, 1979, Agência de Informação de Moçambique, *Information Bulletin* 39 (1979), supp. 6.

43. Marcelino dos Santos, interview, Maputo, August 2, 1977.

44. Allen and Barbara Isaacman, "Mozambique Tells Big Powers: 'Stay on Your Own Blocs,'" *Christian Science Monitor*, November 18, 1980.

45. Quoted in John S. Saul, *The State and Revolution in Eastern Africa* (New York: Monthly Review Press, 1979), 443.

46. Frank Wisner to Graça Machel, October 22, 1986, CDSM, folder 4.

47. See Stephen A. Emerson, *The Battle for Mozambique: The Frelimo-Renamo Struggle, 1977–1992* (Solihull, UK: Helion, 2014).

48. For documentation of these abuses, see Robert Gersony, *Summary of Mozambican Refugee Accounts of Principally Conflict-Related Experience in Mozambique* (Washington, DC: Department of State, Bureau for Refugee Programs, 1988).

49. Vernácio Leone, interview, Estima, May 19, 1998.

50. Their accounts are confirmed in Gersony, *Summary of Mozambican Refugee Accounts*, and William Minter, *Apartheid's Contras: An Inquiry into the Roots of War in Angola and Mozambique* (London: Zed Press, 1994), which also documents coercive mechanisms used by RENAMO to prevent desertions and intimidate the population under its control.

51. Emerson, *Battle for Mozambique*, 165.

52. RENAMO's leader, Afónso Dhlakama, boasted to Portuguese journalists that South African defense minister Magnus Malan had made him a colonel and assured him that his army was now part of the South African Defense Force. Colin Legum, "The Counter Revolutionaries in Southern Africa: The Challenge of the Mozambique National Resistance," *Third World Reports* (March 1983): 13.

53. José Luís Cabaço, interview, June 11, 2018.

54. Gersony, *Summary of Mozambique Refugee Accounts*.

55. Sérgio Chichava, "'They Can Kill Us but We Won't Go to the Communal Villages!': Peasants and the Policy of 'Socialisation of the Countryside' in Zambezia," *Kronos* 39, no. 1 (January 2013): 112–30; Dinerman, *Revolution, Counter-revolution*, 122–26; Christian Geffray, *A causa das armas: Antropologia da guerra contemporânea em Moçambique* (Porto: Afrontamento, 1991).

Chapter 7: The Unraveling of Mozambique's Socialist Revolution, 1983–86

1. Margaret Hall and Tom Young, *Confronting Leviathan: Mozambique since Independence* (Athens: Ohio University Press, 1997), 156–57.

2. Prakash Ratilal, interview, March 23, 2019.

3. M. Anne Pitcher, *Transforming Mozambique: The Politics of Privatization, 1975–2000* (Cambridge: Cambridge University Press, 2002), 103–6.

4. "Report from the Commission for Economic and Social Directives: Frelimo Fourth Party Congress, 1983," reproduced in Allen Isaacman and Barbara Isaacman, *Mozambique: From Colonialism to Revolution* (Boulder, CO: Westview, 1983), 157.

5. Allen Isaacman, "Mozambique Rethinks Marxism, Encourages Private Enterprise," *Christian Science Monitor*, June 15, 1983.

6. "Report from the Commission," 198, 200.

7. Isaacman, "Mozambique Rethinks Marxism."

8. Pitcher, *Transforming Mozambique*, 106.

9. José Luis Cabaço, interview, June 13, 2018.

10. Pitcher, *Transforming Mozambique*, 117.

11. Samora Machel, *Establishing People's Power to Serve the Masses* (Dar es Salaam: Tanzania Publishing House, 1977), 7.

12. Samora Machel, interview, May 7, 1979.

13. Hall and Young, *Confronting Leviathan*, 75.

14. Samora Machel, "Make Beira the Starting-Point for an Organizational Offensive," in Munslow, *Samora Machel*, 73.

15. Teodato Hunguana, interview, June 21, 2018.

16. Quoted in Benedito Luís Machava, "The Morality of Revolution: Urban Cleanup Campaigns, Reeducation Camps, and Citizenship in Socialist Mozambique (1974–1988)" (PhD diss., University of Michigan, 2018), 107.

17. Ibid., 112.

18. Paulo Zucula, interview, Maputo, March 13, 2019.

19. Machava, "Morality of Revolution," 113.

20. Ibid., 15.

21. See, for example, João M. Cabrita, *Mozambique: The Tortuous Road to Democracy* (New York: Palgrave, 2000), 96.

22. Machava, "Morality of Revolution," 15.

23. Carmen Zucula, interview, Maputo, March 16, 2019.

24. Anonymous interview, Maputo, March 28, 2019.

25. Arlindo Chilundo, interview, Maputo, March 9, 2019.

26. Teodato Hunguana, interview, June 21, 2018.

27. Machava, "Morality of Revolution," 154.

28. António Alves Gomes, interview, June 21, 2018.

29. Personal communication from Paul Fauvet, Maputo, July 10, 2019.

30. António Alves Gomes, interview, June 21, 2018.

31. Ibid.

32. José Luís Cabaço, interview, June 13, 2018.

33. António Alves Gomes, interview, June 21, 2018

34. José Luís Cabaço, interview, June 11, 2018.

35. Ibid.; António Alves Gomes, interview, June 21, 2018

36. Oscar Monteiro, interview, Matola, March 15, 2019.

37. Samora Machel's closing statement at the signing of the Nkomati Accord, March 16, 1984, authors' collection.

38. Nyerere had previously told Monteiro that he understood Frelimo had few options and that it was not in the interest of independent Africa for Mozambique to be destroyed just so the ANC could engage in symbolic hit-and-run attacks (Oscar Monteiro, interview, March 15, 2019).

39. Paul Fauvet and Marcelo Mosse, *Carlos Cardoso: Telling the Truth in Mozambique* (Cape Town: Double Storey, 2003), 127.

40. Testimony of João Honwana to Truth and Reconciliation Commission, n.d., South African Historical Archives, file AL2878_BO1.75.01.29.01.

41. Oscar Monteiro, interview, March 15, 2019.

42. On South Africa's military support, see Hall and Young, *Confronting Leviathan*, 115–57.

43. Alice Dinerman, *Revolution, Counter-revolution and Revisionism in Post-colonial Africa: The Case of Mozambique, 1975–1994* (London: Routledge, 2015), 59.

44. William Finnegan, *A Complicated War: The Harrowing of Mozambique* (Berkeley: University of California Press, 1992), 142.

45. Jacinto Veloso, *Memórias em voo rasante* (Maputo: JV Editores, 2011), 159–94.

46. Anonymous interview.

47. Oscar Monteiro, interview, March 26, 2019.

48. José Luís Cabaço, interview, June 13, 2019.

49. Olívia Machel, interview, March 7, 2019.

50. Olívia, Jucelina, and Ornila Machel, joint interview.

51. Anonymous interview.

Chapter 8: Who Killed Samora?

1. *Diário de Moçambique,* October 22, 1986.

2. Jeremy Gavron, "Emotional Funeral for President Machel," *Daily Telegraph* (London), October 29, 1986.

3. *Tempo* (Maputo), November 23, 1986.

4. These are contained in "Telex, Cartas dos Paises Socialistas Sobre o Morte de Samora Machel," 1986, CDSM, folder 4.

5. Letter of condolence from Coretta Scott King to Graça Machel, October 27, 1987, CDSM, folder 4.

6. Godwin Matatu, "Machel's Mourners Snub Botha's Funeral Plea," *Observer* (London), October 26, 1986.

7. Christie, *Samora Machel: A Biography. (*London: Zed Press, 1988), xvii.

8. *Independent* (Lusaka), 22 October, 1986.

9. Lawrence Hamburger, interview, Cape Town, February 29, 2019.

10. *Diário de Moçambique,* 22 October 1982, 22.

11. Paul Fauvet and Marcelo Mosse, *Carlos Cardoso: Telling the Truth in Mozambique* (Cape Town: Double Storey, 2003), 156.

12. Daniel L. Douek, "New Light on the Samora Machel Assassination: 'I Realized That It Was No Accident,'" *Third World Quarterly* 38, no. 9 (2017): 2050–51.

13. Testimony of João Honwana, n.d., 14, SAHA, file AL2878_B01.5.75.01.29.01.

14. Fauvet and Mosse, *Carlos Cardoso*, 156.

15. Testimony of João Honwana, n.d., 10, SAHA, file AL2878_B01.5.75.01.29.01.

16. Fauvet and Mosse, *Carlos Cardoso*, 159.

17. Douek, "New Light," 2056.

18. Another objective for the meeting was to pressure Zaire's president Mobutu Sese Seko to stop supporting UNITA, an Angolan opposition group linked to both Pretoria and the United States.

19. Fauvet and Mosse, *Carlos Cardoso*, 162.

20. Douek, "New Light," 2055.

21. Fauvet and Mosse, *Carlos Cardoso*, 164.

22. Testimony of João Honwana, n.d., 6–7, SAHA, file AL2878_B01.5.75.01.29.01.

23. This material is located in the South Africa History Archives (SAHA), file AL2878_B01.5.75.01.29.01–29.09. For an informative exploration of these documents, see Douek, "New Light."

24. Fauvet and Mosse, *Carlos Cardoso*, 156.

25. Pretoria dismissed the claims regarding a beacon, which it labeled "communist propaganda," in an hour-long TV documentary produced by military intelligence and psychological officers and aired by the South African Broadcasting Company in 1987 (Douek, "New Light," 2056–58).

26. Testimony of João Honwana, n.d., 5, SAHA, file AL2878_B01.5.75.01.29.01.

27. Fauvet and Mosse, *Carlos Cardoso*, 166–67.

28. Ibid., 170.

29. Douek, "New Light," 2055.

30. Ibid., 2056. See testimony of Willem Oostuizen, n.d., 300–305, SAHA, file AL2878_B01.5.75.01.29.09.

31. Testimony of J. H. Basson, n.d., 166–67, SAHA, file AL2878_B01.5.75.01.29.09.

32. Testimony of João Honwana, n.d., 7, SAHA, file AL2878_B01.5.75.01.29.01.

33. Douek, "New Light," 2058.

34. Ibid., 2050.

35. Testimony of Debra Patta, n.d., 146, SAHA, file AL2878_B01.5.75.01.29.04.

36. Ibid., 45, 142.

37. Ibid., 116.

38. According to a radio-monitoring expert who was based in Swaziland at the time, it is possible that the Maputo VOR was functioning properly but was simply overridden by a more powerful signal (personal communication with William Minter, Washington, D.C., January 14, 2019).

39. António Alves Gomes, interview, Maputo, March 12, 2019.

Chapter 9: The Political Afterlife of Samora and the Politics of Memory

1. M. Anne Pitcher, "Forgetting from Above and Memory from Below: Strategies of Legitimation and Struggle in Post-socialist Mozambique," *Africa: Journal of the International African Institute* 76, no. 1 (2006): 96–98.

2. Maria-Benedita Basto, "The Writings of the National Anthem in Independent Mozambique: Fictions of the Subject-People," *Kronos* 39, no. 1 (2013): 193.

3. Perhaps the most memorable line in this version was "we are soldiers of the people fighting the bourgeoisie" (personal communication from Paul Fauvet, Maputo, July 13, 2019).

4. Amélia Neves de Souto, "Memory and Identity in the History of Frelimo: Some Research Themes," *Kronos* 39, no. 1 (2013): 289.

5. *Domingos* (Maputo), October 29, 1986; *Njigniritane*, November 2, 1986; *Domingos* (Maputo), October 20, 1997; *Demos* (Maputo), October 15, 1997; *Zambeze* (Beira), June 26, 2003.

6. *Savana* (Maputo), April 18, 2004; *Domingos* (Maputo), October 22, 2006; *Notícias* (Maputo), October 17, 2006; *Notícias* (Maputo), October 8, 2016.

7. José Luís Cabaço, interview, June 21, 2018.

8. Souto, "Memory and Identity," 292–95.

9. Quoted in Pitcher, "Forgetting from Above," 104.

10. Khalid Shamis, "The Mbuzini Memorial: A Film Project" (paper presented at the conference" The Living Legacies of Samora Machel," Center for Humanities Research, University of Western Cape, February 12, 2019).

11. David Hoile, *Mozambique: Propaganda, Myth and Reality* (London: Mozambique Institute, 1991); Victor Igreja, "Frelimo's Political Ruling through Violence and Memory in Postcolonial Mozambique," *Journal of Southern African Studies* 36, no. 4 (December 2010): 781–99; Sérgio Chichava, "'They Can Kill Us but We Won't Go to the Communal Villages!': Peasants and the Policy of 'Socialisation of the Countryside' in Zambezia," *Kronos* 39, no. 1 (January 2013): 112–30.

12. Janne Rantala, "'Hidrunisa Samora': Invocations of a Dead Political Leader in Maputo Rap," *Journal of Southern African Studies* 42, no. 6 (November 2016): 1162.

13. Ibid., 1174.

14. Ibid., 1172.

15. Azagaia, interview, Maputo, March 30, 2019.

16. Rantala, "'Hidrunisa Samora,'" 1162.

17. António Alves Gomes, interview, June 21, 2018.

18. José Luís Cabaço, interview, June 21, 2018.

19. Alpheus Manghezi, "Samora Machel: Man of the People," in *Samora: Man of the People,* ed. Antonio Sopa (Maputo: Maguezo Editores, 2001), 135.

20. This *mapiko* song from Shitunda was composed by songmaster Bernardino Juakali Namba, who had been arrested in 1960 for singing a song on the Mueda massacre. Recorded in Cabo Delgado, 2008, by Paolo Israel; Israel's translation.

21. Mang'anyamu Matambalale was an animal masquerade group. Recorded in Cabo Delgado, 2005, by Paolo Israel. In Paolo Israel, *In Step with the Times: Mapiko Masquerades of Mozambique* (Athens: Ohio University Press, 2014), 229.

22. Lingundumbwe Mbwidi (Nangade) was one of the last women's groups to perform historical dances. Recorded in Cabo Delgado, 2004, by Paolo Israel.

23. Musaemura Zimunya, "In Memory of Machel," in *Samora! Tribute to a Revolutionary,* ed. Chenjerai Hove, Gibson Mandishona, and Musaemura Zimunya (Harare: Zimbabwe Writers Union and Zimbabwe Newspapers Ltd., 1986), 14. *Braai* is Afrikaans for barbecue.

24. This was part of a conversation Allen had with a taxi driver who was transporting him around Maputo in May 2018.

25. Mantchiyani Samora Machel, *My love: A nossa forma de estar e a cegueira deliberada* (Maputo: Kapicua Livros e Multi-média Maputo, 2017).

26. Two days before our scheduled departure for Beira to speak to critics of Samora, Cyclone Ida devastated the city and much of the surrounding region, making our trip impossible.

27. Janna Rantala, "'*Chambocadas todos ali*': Ambivalence of Samora and His Time in Mozambican Rap" (paper presented at the conference "The Living Legacies of Samora Machel," Center for Humanities Research, University of Western Cape, February 12, 2019).

Conclusion: Samora's Life Revisited

1. *Nóticias*, April 9, 1984, 1.

Recommended Reading

Reference Books

Christie, Iain. *Samora Machel: A Biography*. London: Zed Press, 1988.

Darch, Colin. *Historical Dictionary of Mozambique*. Lanham, MD: Rowman and Littlefield, 2019.

Gomes, António Alves, and Albie Sachs, eds. *Samora Machel*. Cape Town: African Lives, 2018.

Le Fanu, Sarah. *S is for Samora: A Lexical Biography of Samora Machel and the Mozambican Dream*. Durban: University of Kwa-Zulu Natal Press, 2012.

Mondlane, Eduardo. *The Struggle for Mozambique*. London: Zed Press, 1983.

Newitt, Malyn. *A History of Mozambique*. Bloomington: Indiana University Press, 1995.

Sopa, António, ed. *Samora: Man of the People*. Maputo: Maguezo Editores, 2001.

Souto, Amélia Neves de, and António Sopa, eds. *Samora Machel: Bibliografia (1970–1986)*. Maputo: Centro de Estudos Africanos, Universidade Eduardo Mondlane, 1996.

Memoirs

Bragança, Sílvia. *Aquino de Bragança: Batalhas ganhas, sonhos a continuar*. Maputo: Ndjira, 2009.

Caliate, Zeca. *A odisseia de um guerrilheiro*. Self-published, CreateSpace, 2014.

Chipande, Alberto Joaquim. *Como eu vivo a minha história*. Maputo: Kadimah, 2018.

Ferrão, Valeriano. *Embaixador nos USA*. Maputo: Ndjira, 2007.

Chissano, Joaquim Alberto. *Vidas, lugares e tempos*. Maputo: Texto Editores, 2010.

Honwana, Luís Bernardo. *A velha casa de madeira e zinco*. Maputo: Alcance, 2017.

Manghezi, Nadja. *The Maputo Connection: ANC Life in the World of Frelimo*. Cape Town: Jacana, 2009.

Martins, Helder. *Porquê Sakrani? Memórias dum médico duma guerrilha esquecida*. Maputo: Editorial Terceiro Milénio, 2001.

Mondlane, Janet Rae, ed. *O eco da tua voz: Cartas editadas de Eduardo Mondlane*. Vol. 1. Maputo: Imprensa Universitária UEM, 2007.

Monteiro, Óscar. *De todos se faz um país*. Maputo: Associação dos Escritores Moçambicanos, 2012.

Nihia, Eduardo Silva. *M'toto: Combatente pela liberdade*. Maputo: Imprensa Universitária UEM, 2016.

Pachinuapa, Raimundo, ed. *Memórias da revolução, 1962–1974: Colectânea de entrevistas de combatentes da luta de libertação nacional*. Vol. 1. Maputo: Centro de Pesquisa da História da Luta de Libertação Nacional, 2011.

Pelembe, Joao Facitela. *Lutei pela pátria: Memórias de um combatente da luta pela libertação nacional*. Maputo: self-published, 2012.

Veloso, Jacinto. *Memories at Low Altitude: The Autobiography of a Mozambican Security Chief*. Cape Town: Zebra Press, 2012.

Websites

JSTOR, Struggles for Freedom Southern Africa. https://www.aluka.org/struggles.

Mozambique History Net. Colin Darch, ed. http://www.mozambiquehistory.net.

Academic Studies

Adam, Yussuf. *Escapar aos dentes do crocodilo e cair na boca do leopardo: Trajectoria de Moçambique pós-colonial (1975–1990)*. Maputo: Promédia, 2005.

Alpers, Edward A. "Islam in the Service of Colonialism? Portuguese Strategy during the Armed Liberation Struggle in Mozambique." *Lusotopie*, no. 6 (1999): 165–84.

Bowen, Merle L. *The State against the Peasantry: Rural Struggles in Colonial and Postcolonial Mozambique*. Charlottesville: University Press of Virginia, 2000.

Cruz e Silva, Teresa. *Protestant Churches and the Formation of Political Consciousness in Southern Mozambique (1930–1974)*. Basel: P. Schlettwein, 2001.

Darch, Colin. "Are There Warlords in Provincial Mozambique? Questions of the Social Base of MNR Banditry." *Review of African Political Economy*, no. 45/46 (1989): 34–49.

Darch, Colin, and David Hedges. "Political Rhetoric in the Transition to Mozambican Independence: Samora Machel in Beira, June 1975." *Kronos* 39, no. 1 (2013): 32–65.

Dhada, Mustafah. *The Portuguese Massacre of Wiriyamu in Colonial Mozambique, 1964–2013*. New York: Bloomsbury Academic, 2016.

Dinerman, Alice. *Revolution, Counter-revolution and Revisionism in Post-colonial Africa: The Case of Mozambique, 1975–1994*. London: Routledge, 2015.

Douek, Daniel L. "New Light on the Samora Machel Assassination: 'I Realized That It Was No Accident,'" *Third World Quarterly* 38, no. 9 (2017): 2045–65.

Emerson, Stephen A. *The Battle for Mozambique: The Frelimo-Renamo Struggle, 1977–1992*. Solihull, UK: Helion, 2014.

Finnegan, William. *A Complicated War: The Harrowing of Mozambique*. Berkeley: University of California Press, 1996.

Funada-Classen, Sayaka. *The Origins of War in Mozambique: A History of Unity and Division*. Oxford: African Minds, 2013.

Geffray, Christian. *A causa das armas: Antropologia da guerra contemporânea em Moçambique*. Translated by Adelaide Odete Ferreira. Porto: Afrontamento, 1991. Originally published as *La cause des armes au Mozambique: Anthropologie d'une guerre civile* (Paris: Karthala, 1990).

Hall, Margaret, and Tom Young. *Confronting Leviathan: Mozambique since Independence*. Athens: Ohio University Press, 1997.

Hanlon, Joseph. *Mozambique: The Revolution under Fire*. London: Zed Books, 1984.

Isaacman, Allen. *Cotton Is the Mother of Poverty: Peasants, Work, and Rural Struggle in Colonial Mozambique, 1938–1961*. Portsmouth, NH: Heinemann, 2004.

Isaacman, Allen, and Barbara Isaacman. *Dams, Displacement, and the Delusion of Development: Cahora Bassa and Its Legacies in Mozambique, 1965–2007*. Athens: Ohio University Press, 2013.

———. *Mozambique: From Colonialism to Revolution*. Boulder, CO: Westview, 1983.

———. *The Tradition of Resistance in Mozambique: Anti-colonial Activity in the Zambesi Valley, 1850–1921*. Berkeley: University of California Press, 1976.

Manning, Carrie. *The Politics of Peace in Mozambique: Postconflict Democratization, 1992–2000*. Westport: Greenwood, 2002.

Marcum, John A. *Conceiving Mozambique*. Cham, Switzerland: Palgrave Macmillan, 2018.

Marshall, Judith. *Literacy, Power, and Democracy in Mozambique: The Governance of Learning from Colonization to the Present*. Boulder, CO: Westview, 1993.

Matusse, Renato. *Coronel-General Fernando Matavele: De cidadão vulgar a patriota invulgar*. Maputo: Texto Editores, 2012.

Mboa, Matias. *Memórias da luta clandestina*. Maputo: Marimbique, 2009.

Minter, William. *Apartheid's Contras: An Inquiry into the Roots of War in Angola and Mozambique*. London, Zed Press, 1994.

Munslow, Barry. *Mozambique: The Revolution and Its Origins*. London: Longman, 1983.

———, ed. *Samora Machel, an African Revolutionary: Selected Speeches and Writings*. London: Zed Press, 1995.

Newitt, Malyn. *A Short History of Mozambique.* London: Oxford, 2017.

Roesch, Otto. "Renamo and the Peasantry in Southern Mozambique: A View from Gaza Province." *Canadian Journal of African Studies* 26, no. 3 (1992): 462–84.

Saul, John S., ed. *A Difficult Road: The Transition to Socialism in Mozambique.* New York: Monthly Review Press, 1985.

———. *The State and Revolution in Eastern Africa.* New York: Monthly Review Press, 1979.

Sheldon, Kathleen. *Pounders of Grain: A History of Women, Work, and Politics in Mozambique.* Portsmouth, NH: Heinemann, 2002.

Tembe, Joel das Neves, ed. *História da luta de libertação nacional.* Vol. 1. Maputo: Ministério dos Combatentes, Direcção Nacional da História, 2014.

———, ed. "Uhuru ni Kazi: Recapturing MANU Nationalism through the Archive." *Kronos* 39, no. 1 (November 2013): 257–79.

Vines, Alex. *RENAMO: From Terrorism to Democracy in Mozambique?* 2nd rev. ed. London: James Currey, 1996.

Wilson, K. B. "Cults of Violence and Counter-violence in Mozambique." *Journal of Southern African Studies* 18, no. 3 (September 1992): 527–82.

Young, Tom. "The MNR/RENAMO: External and Internal Dynamics." *African Affairs* 89, no. 357 (October 1990): 491–509.

Index